KEY IDEAS

Literature

Brenda Downes

TEACH YOURSELF BOOKS

For UK orders: please contact Bookpoint Ltd, 130 Milton Park, Abingdon, Oxon OX14 4SB. Telephone: (44) 01235 827720, Fax: (44) 01235 400454. Lines are open from 9.00–18.00, Monday to Saturday, with a 24-hour message answering service. Email address: orders@bookpoint.co.uk

For U.S.A. order enquiries: please contact McGraw-Hill Customer Services, P.O. Box 545, Blackllick, OH 43004-05455, U.S.A. Telephone: 1-800-722-4726. Fax: 1-614-755-5645.

For Canada order enquiries: please contact McGraw-Hill Ryerson Ltd., 300 Water St, Whitby, Ontario L1N 9B6, Canada. Telephone: 905 430 5000. Fax: 905 430 5020.

Long renowned as the authoritative source for self-guided learning – with more than 30 million copies sold worldwide – the *Teach Yourself* series includes over 300 titles in the fields of languages, crafts, hobbies, business and education.

British Library Cataloguing in Publication Data
A catalogue record for this title is available from The British Library.

Library of Congress Catalog Card Number: On file

First published in UK 2002 by Hodder Headline Plc, 338 Euston Road, London, NW1 3BH.

First published in US 2002 by Contemporary Books, A Division of The McGraw-Hill Companies, 4255 West Touhy Avenue, Lincolnwood (Chicago), Illinois 60712-1975, U.S.A.

The 'Teach Yourself' name and logo are registered trade marks of Hodder & Stoughton Ltd.

Cover design by Mike Stones

Typeset by Transet Limited, Coventry, England.
Printed in Great Britain for Hodder & Stoughton Educational, a division of Hodder Headline Plc, 338 Euston Road, London NW1 3BH by Cox & Wyman Ltd, Reading, Berkshire.

Impression number	10 9 8 7 6 5 4 3 2 1
Year	2007 2006 2005 2004 2003 2002

Contents

Introduction

Welcome to the **Teach Yourself 101 Key Ideas** series. We hope that you will find both this book and others in the series to be useful, interesting and informative. The purpose of the series is to provide an introduction to a wide range of subjects, in a way that is entertaining and easy to absorb.

Each book contains 101 short accounts of key ideas or terms which are regarded as central to that subject. The accounts are presented in alphabetical order for ease of reference. All of the books in the series are written in order to be meaningful whether or not you have previous knowledge of the subject. They will be useful to you whether you are a general reader, are on a pre-university course, or have just started at university.

We have designed the series to be a combination of a text book and a dictionary. We felt that many text books are too long for easy reference, while the entries in dictionaries are often too short to provide sufficient

detail. The **Teach Yourself 101 Key Ideas** series gives the best of both worlds! Here are books that you do not have to read cover to cover, or in any set order. Dip into them when you need to know the meaning of a term, and you will find a short, but comprehensive account which will be of real help with those essays and assignments. The terms are described in a straightforward way with a careful selection of academic words thrown in for good measure!

So if you need a quick and inexpensive introduction to a subject, **Teach Yourself 101 Key Ideas** is for you. And incidentally, if you have any suggestions about this book or the series, do let us know. It would be great to hear from you.

Best wishes with your studies!

Paul Oliver
Series Editor

Acmeism

The name of the style is taken from a Greek word meaning pinnacle or utmost height. A group of young Russian poets formed the Poets' Guild in 1911 and published the magazine *Apollon.* They believed that poets should be craftsmen, not prophets. Poets writing within the movement wanted to depict the world in as real terms as possible, using language precisely and logically to give a clear set of representations. The Acmeists rejected both symbolism and mysticism, which they felt allowed vagueness.

The Acmeists had a great impact on Russian literature before the First World War, but their collective opposition to the revolution and conservative politics led to a loss of popularity during the 1920s. They failed to conform to the doctrine of Socialist Realism after 1934 and attracted official disapproval, which led to publishing bans and prison sentences.

Nikolai Stephanovich Gumilev wrote *The Path of the Conquistadors* (1905), which became a founding text of the school. Gumilev opposed the Bolshevik revolution in 1916, and was executed for conspiracy after a plot to restore the monarchy in 1921. His wife, Anna Akhmatova, wrote mainly love poems within the principles of Acmeism. She published little after 1922.

Osip Mandelstam wrote two major collections, *Stone* (1913) and *Tristia* (1922). His work combined knowledge from his classical education with the precision and brevity demanded by the group. Although an opponent of the revolution, his work continued to be published, until he was arrested and exiled to Siberia after publicly criticizing Josef Stalin in 1934. Mandelstam continued to write and was arrested again in 1938. He died in a labour camp. His wife, Nadezhda Yakovlevna Khazina, wrote two volumes of memoirs, *Hope Against Hope* (1971) and *Hope Abandoned* (1974), neither of which were published in Russia.

see also...

Socialist Realism

Adaptations

To adapt is to make something suitable for a new need. Thus a chair could be adapted to make a stool and a book could prop up a table that has legs of different heights.

The usual reason for adapting a book is to change its form so that the story can be presented to audiences in another medium. Most commonly, novels are adapted for the stage, television or films. It is not usually possible or necessary to include the whole of the original text in any adaptations. This is partly because electronic media communicate with audiences in a different way, which causes large parts of the original text to become redundant. They offer additional information, which is not available on a printed page. Pictures and sound replace much of the description which is necessary in a book. A member of the theatre, television or cinema audience can see and hear what is happening, whereas readers have to rely on the writer's choice of words to help them to imagine people, places and events.

It is not only the best loved stories which are adapted for other media. An adaptation can reach a wider audience than most books. An example is Thomas Keneally's *Schindler's Ark* (1982), which was filmed as *Schindler's List* in 1994. Audiences are drawn from: people interested in different interpretations of a much-loved story; people lacking the time or capability to read the original text; people new to the story; and even those who want to prove to themselves that an adaptation is never as good as the original book.

There is also a tradition in some countries of adapting books for a different audience from that which was originally targeted. Sometimes books written for adults are simplified and shortened for younger readers, for example, Jonathan Swift's *Gulliver's Travels* (1726). Some books are adapted for audiotape. In both cases, the original text is shortened considerably and this process is called abridgement.

Agitprop

This term was used originally to describe drama or films which were created with the specific intention of inducing audiences to participate in political action or agitation. These works were originally produced in Russia in the years following the revolution after the Department of Agitation and Propaganda was set up in 1920. This department had responsibility for ensuring that the principles of the revolution were spread. As the population was mostly illiterate, the emphasis was on delivering the message through live theatre and film. Special trains equipped with film making and exhibition facilities travelled across Russia with a brief to spread the ideology of the revolution. The poet and playwright Vladimir Mayakovsky wrote a verse play in 1918 called *Mystery Bouffe* in which the working class battle with and defeat the upper class and establish a workers' paradise.

By the 1930s the term was used to describe any literature or art which encouraged a left wing analysis of society, and could be thought to promote action on the behalf of readers or audiences. Some of the work of Berthold Brecht included what he called 'teaching plays' which derived their style from Russian agitprop. In *He Who Says Yes and He Who Says No* (1930), he offered audiences pieces which discussed specific political issues.

During the 1960s and 1970s, agitprop productions became popular in Europe and the USA. A desire to change social structures by the post-war generation led to a blossoming of oppositional writing and performance, for example, the Wooster Group and the People Show.

A current development is Theatre-for-Development, which exists in Third World countries. Groups involved work on exploratory and improvisational pieces with the explicit intention of enabling participants to analyse their lives and devise and implement strategies for change.

see also...

Epic Theatre

3

Alienation

he creation of an 'alienation effect' is sometimes used by writers to prevent the reader or audience from identifying with or trusting the narrative or action of a novel or play. Writers may achieve this effect in several ways. Disruptions to the narrative such as flashbacks and the pre-figuring of events which have yet to occur in the narrative, can have an alienating effect on the reader, who becomes temporarily confused by the non-linear narrative style. A sudden mood change or the introduction of non-realistic events have a similar effect. Many modernist stream of consciousness novels have the effect of alienating the reader from close identification with characters.

Fyodor Dostoyevsky's *Notes from the Underground* (1864) and the Epic Theatre of Bertold Brecht both use alienation techniques. The Czech playwright and novelist Milan Kundera used alienation in *Jacques and His Master* (1981) and in his experimental novel *The Unbearable Lightness of Being* (1987).

There is a tradition of creating characters who are alienated from their own fictional worlds. Lemuel Gulliver in Jonathan Swift's *Gulliver's Travels* (1726) is alienated from the societies which he visits and also from his fictional home.

Every novel by the Czech writer Franz Kafka portrayed lonely victims who cannot understand the events in which they are caught up. This is especially true of Gregor, whose alienation is symbolized by a physical transformation in *Metamorphosis* (1915). Albert Camus's novels, especially *The Outsider* (1942) and *The Plague* (1947), have deeply alienated characters, as do the plays of other absurdist and surrealist dramatists. Anthony Burgess's *A Clockwork Orange* (1962) examines the effects of alienation, while Russell Hoban's *The Medusa Frequency* (1987) portrays a character who is pitched into a confusing and alienating sequence of events.

see also...

Altered States; Magical Realism; Stream of Consciousness; Surrealism

Allegory

An allegory is an extended metaphor in which characters, objects, incidents and descriptions carry a full set of meanings in addition to their literal meanings. The earliest examples of allegorical writing can be found among Aesop's Fables.

In John Bunyan's *The Pilgrim's Progress* (1678), the chief character, Christian, is not simply a character but has a second set of meanings which allow him to stand for, or symbolize, Christianity itself. Christian's adventures also have a second set of meanings that symbolize humankind's journey through life to Heaven and the conflict between good and evil. There was often a moral lesson hidden within an apparently simple tale, as in *The Pilgrim's Progress.*

Another common device used in allegorical writing is 'personification', which is a device whereby human feelings and characteristics are attributed to ideas, objects and non-human beings. By treating such things as characters, abstract qualities can be portrayed and explained in a more concrete way.

Edmund Spenser's *The Faerie Queen* (1590–96) is an allegorical tale about the reign of Elizabeth I, in which she and her knights represent desirable qualities.

Although allegorical prose writing was most popular during the Middle Ages, there are many later examples. Nathaniel Hawthorne's *The Marble Faun* (1860) and Virginia Woolf's *Between The Acts* (1941) are both allegorical. Other examples are J.G. Farrell's *Troubles* (1970) and *The Siege of Krishnapur* (1973) in which Farrell uses allegory to discuss the complex political issues. In Jim Crace's *The Gift of Stones* (1998), a novel set in the Stone Age becomes an allegory of modern economics. In *Arcadia* (1992), Crace sets the story around the building of a shopping centre and uses the characters' positions to explore issues about the free market economy.

Allegory is still most often found in poetry, which easily lends itself to the extended metaphor.

see also...

Imagery; Metaphysical

Altered States

Many fictional characters live their lives in an altered state, either voluntarily or involuntarily. The authors themselves have, for the most part, had direct personal experience of the states they describe, but this is not necessarily always true. The fiction is an attempt to offer readers an insight into life outside mainstream cultural practices and the transgression of social rules. Some writers consider only the personal consequences, while others consider the impact on society as a whole.

Of the many books about alcoholism, *Hangover Square* by Patrick Hamilton (1941); *The Lost Weekend* by Charles Jackson (1945); *Under The Volcano* by Malcolm Lowry (1947); and Evelyn Waugh's *The Ordeal of Gilbert Pinfold* (1957) are among the best known. *Ironweed* (1983), the fourth part of William Kennedy's sequence of novels, chronicles the effect of alcohol on the lives of the Phelan family.

Since Thomas De Quincey famously consumed laudanum and wrote *Confessions of an English Opium Eater* (1821), writers have experimented with and written about drug-taking experiences. Aldous Huxley conceived a society controlled by the government through the use of drugs in *Brave New World* (1932), and in the utopian novel *Island* (1962) the drug-taking was purely voluntary. Hunter S. Thompson's *Fear and Loathing in Las Vegas* (1972) and the novels of William Burroughs are about addictions and attempts to break them. Recently, J.G. Ballard's *Cocaine Nights* (1997) and Irvine Welsh's *Trainspotting* (1993) and *Ecstasy* (1997) consider the impact of new drugs on a new generation.

Twentieth-century novels about mental health and illness and its treatment and solutions include Sylvia Plath's *The Bell Jar* (1963) and Ken Kesey's *One Flew Over The Cuckoos Nest* (1962). Doris Lessing's *Briefing for a Descent into Hell* (1971) and Janice Galloway's *The Trick is to Keep Breathing* (1990) are about surviving mental illness.

see also...

Alienation

Angry Young Men

This term is used to describe a group of English playwrights and novelists. At the end of the Second World War, a Labour government was elected in England and opportunities for higher education became available to lower middle-class people for the first time. By the mid-1950s, the first generation of working-class graduates were ready to build careers, only to discover that the pre-war social structures had not changed. They were not accepted in the jobs and social circles to which their education entitled them, because education alone did not allow them to move up the English class structure. Many used literature to express and publicize their anger, disillusionment, discontent and frustration with the slow pace of social change in post-war Britain.

John Osborne is probably the best known of this group. His play *Look Back in Anger* (1956), traces the frustration of Jimmy Porter, a working-class graduate, during his marriage to Alison, a colonel's daughter. The play explores class and personal conflict in ways which had never been shown before on the English stage. He also wrote *The Entertainer* (1957) and *Inadmissible Evidence* (1964). Osborne's last play, *Deja vu* (1991), was a sequel to *Look Back in Anger*, with the same characters. Kingsley Amis turned anger to humour in the novel *Lucky Jim* (1954), in which he satirized the pressure on people who tried to 'better themselves' and move through the class system. Amis returned to this idea in other novels.

Whereas Osborne and Amis wrote about the problems of the aspiring middle class, and were graduates, Alan Sillitoe wrote about the working class. He was self-educated and had only been able to give up his job to write full-time after his novel, *Saturday Night and Sunday Morning* (1958), and an anthology of short stories, *The Loneliness of the Long Distance Runner* (1959), had been published. David Storey's *This Sporting Life* (1960) and Colin Wilson's *The Outsider* (1956) are often included in this group.

Banned, Exiled and Imprisoned Writers

Fiction has been banned by many governments throughout history. Punishment for those who disseminate ideas which governments wish to suppress has included exile and imprisonment. Fiction can be a powerful ideological tool and novelists, poets and playwrights have suffered alongside journalists and non-fiction writers. Some writers produce allegorical or satirical works in an attempt to disguise criticism of their governments.

Many writers suffered in the USSR. The Bolshevik Alexandra Kollontai, author of *Love of Worker Bees* (1923), was imprisoned before the revolution. Victor Serge and Alexander Solzenitsyn (*One Day in the Life of Ivan Denisovich*, 1962) were imprisoned, and Joseph Brodsky was imprisoned then exiled to the USA. Brodsky won the Nobel Prize for Literature in 1987. More recently, the Polish poet Czeslaw Milosz, who was awarded the Nobel Prize for Literature in 1980, was exiled to the USA. The Czech playwright, Vaclav Havel, was imprisoned for campaigning against the Soviet Union. He later became president of the Czech Republic.

During war time, writers are often political targets. Arthur Koestler, who wrote *Darkness at Noon* (1940), was imprisoned during the Spanish Civil War. Although many writers and artists went into exile like Rafael Alberti, the poet Federico Garcia Lorca remained in Spain and was executed by fascists.

During the Second World War, imprisoned writers included Primo Levi, who was in Auschwitz. Both Gunter Grass and Ezra Pound were imprisoned by the Allies.

In Nigeria, Ngugi wa Thiong'o, author of *Petals of Blood* (1977), and Wole Soyinka, who won the Nobel Prize in 1986, were imprisoned for criticizing the Government. As recently as 1995, Ken Saro-Wiwa was convicted and hanged in Nigeria. The Chileans, Pablo Neruda and Isabel Allende were forced into exile.

see also...

Dissidence; Satire

Beat Generation

Herbert Hunke (1916–96) coined the term 'beat' to describe himself and his life. He spent years travelling through America during the depression, making notes for novels left unwritten until the end of his life and supporting a heroin habit. When he arrived in New York in the late 1940s he was addicted, exhausted, alienated and drifting through life in post-war America.

In 1947 he met a group of poets and writers who had already imagined a 'New Vision', which would challenge the conformity of post war USA. Their work was rebellious and oppositional, as they rejected the norm of middle class values and commercialism. This group readily embraced Hunke's philosophy and became the most famous voices of the Beat Generation. At one point over a thousand writers were using the style. They produced loose structured free verse and novels. They promoted voluntary poverty, individuality and personal release through jazz, sex, alcohol, drugs and their own interpretations of Buddhism and mysticism.

Much of the material was published by City Lights, which was run by the poet Lawrence Ferlinghetti who wrote *A Coney Island of the Mind* (1958). Some of the work was so challenging that there were attempts to prevent publication. Both Allen Ginsberg's *Howl and Other Poems* (1956) and William Burroughs's novel, *The Naked Lunch* (1959), were the subjects of obscenity trials before eventual publication.

Jack Kerouac wrote several novels, the most famous of which is *On The Road,* written on a continuous roll of paper in three weeks in 1957. Kerouac added a new meaning to beat when he said it was also short for 'beautiful'. Other writers associated with the movement include the poet Gregory Corso (*Gasoline,* 1958) and Gary Snyder (*Riprap,* 1959).

see also...

Underground Poetry

Biographical and Autobiographical Writing

Writing about the lives of real people can be traced back to the ancient Greeks and Romans. Biographies are accounts of real people's lives, written by another person. Autobiographies, which first began to appear in English during the nineteenth-century, are the accounts which people write of their own lives. Both biographies and autobiographies are generally accepted as containing truthful details about past events.

In a biography, truth and detail may be limited by the availability of material, and in an autobiography, the author may deliberately limit the scope of the account. In biography, the relationship of the writer to the subject may influence attitudes to the subject and choices about inclusion and exclusion of material. Some autobiographical works are 'ghost-written', which means that a professional writer has been employed to do the writing. Both kinds of writing are classified as non fiction by publishers, booksellers and libraries.

While it can be argued that all forms of fiction produce episodes from the lives of invented characters, there is a discrete literary genre of fictional biography and autobiography. In such works, the author adopts the non-fiction style to write the life story of an invented character. The style is therefore a pastiche of the genuine biography or autobiography and is usually chosen for its humorous potential.

Laurence Sterne's *Life and Opinions of Tristram Shandy* (1759–67) is fictional autobiography. Virginia Woolf wrote *Flush* (1933), a fictional biography of a dog belonging to Robert and Elizabeth Barratt-Browning. Julian Barnes's *Flaubert's Parrot* (1984) is told through a fictional biographer who is obsessed with the writer Gustave Flaubert. One unusual example is C. Northcote Parkinson's *The Life and Times of Horatio Hornblower* (1970), the fictional biography of a character created by another author, C.S. Forester.

see also...

Diaries

Bloomsbury Group

The name given to a group of British writers, philosophers and artists who used to gather in London during the early years of the twentieth-century. Bloomsbury had become a cultural centre after the building of the British Museum in 1759 and the opening of London University in 1826. By the 1900s the area was well provided with libraries and bookshops but was unfashionable, which made housing affordable.

Although members of the group came from well-established, well-connected and well-educated families, they were regarded as radical and avant-garde. Their work challenged and rejected the restrictive values of Victorian England and influenced the development of English arts and literature. The group included the artists Roger Fry and Duncan Grant, the critic Clive Bell, the philosopher Bertrand Russell and the economist John Maynard Keynes. The writers E. M. Forster, Lytton Strachey and Leonard Woolf still enjoy international acclaim. Two sisters married within this group: Vanessa Bell became an art critic and

Virginia Woolf is recognized as one of the greatest novelists of the century. Virginia and Leonard Woolf set up the Hogarth Press to publish their own work, European novels in translation and the work of many young writers including T. S. Eliot.

Virginia Woolf is the most famous of the Bloomsbury writers. She published nine novels and many volumes of essays, letters and feminist writings. Following the publication of her third novel, *Jacob's Room* (1919), Woolf became established as a modernist writer. In *Mrs Dalloway* (1925) and *The Waves* (1931), she developed experimental techniques. Woolf is best known for a style known as 'stream of consciousness' or 'interior monologue', which presents characters' emotions, memories and impressions in a 'raw' state, running on just as thoughts do and often omitting conventional punctuation.

see also...

Modernism; Stream of Consciousness

Borrowed Characters

Writers often create such compelling characters that other writers feel that further exploration is appropriate. While many novels and poems are based on characters from ancient myths, legends and fables, there is a growing body of modern work which borrows from more recent fiction.

Jean Rhys based her novel *Wide Sargasso Sea* (1966) on the first wife of Mr Rochester, the incarcerated lunatic in Charlotte Brontë's *Jane Eyre* (1847). A series of novels by George MacDonald Fraser borrows the character Flashman from *Tom Brown's Schooldays* (1857) by Thomas Hughes. In Hughes's novel, Flashman is a cowardly bully, whereas the re-working gradually develops him into an almost courageous adventurer.

Scarlett (1992), by Alexandra Ripley, continues the story of Scarlett O'Hara, the heroine of Margaret Mitchell's *Gone With the Wind* (1936). Emma Tennant's *Pemberley* (1993) is a sequel to Jane Austen's *Pride and Prejudice*

(1813). James Wilson borrows characters from Wilkie Collins's *The Moonstone* (1868) in *The Dark Clue* (2001).

Borrowings from William Shakespeare's work are common. While some works are adaptations, sometimes characters are set in their own narratives. Tom Stoppard based his play *Rosencrantz and Guildenstern Are Dead* (1967) on two minor characters from *Hamlet* (1602). Jane Smiley's novel *A Thousand Acres* (1992) re-examines the relationship between a father and his daughters explored by Shakespeare in *King Lear* (1605).

Adaptations of Charles Dickens's novels are very popular, partly due to their complicated plotting. Ruth Alexander, in 1935, finished Dickens's unfinished novel, *The Mystery of Edwin Drood* (1870). Peter Carey based the eponymous hero *Jack Maggs* (1997) on Magwich, the criminal benefactor of Pip, the hero of *Great Expectations* (1860).

see also...

Adaptations

Brat Pack

The 'Brat Pack' is the name given to a group of young New York novelists during the 1980s. Their work reflects and portrays the late twentieth-century 'cool' culture. This was based on the hedonistic lifestyle of the young members of wealthy urban society whose lives involved going to clubs where drugs and alcohol were consumed, and where celebrity was an obsession. Characters are often apparently unaffected by their own actions, which are barely controlled, and sometimes out of control. The characters remain cool, deadpan and remote from their actions, taking no responsibility. Debate has raged about whether these novels promoted immorality and nihilism or whether they were satires about the breakdown of morality at the end of the century. Most authors remain silent in this debate, apart from insisting that their work is fiction.

Brett Easton Ellis has written four novels: *Less Than Zero* (1985), *Rules of Attraction* (1987), *American Psycho* (1991) and *The Informers* (1994). They have been criticized for their characters' violent expressions of dissatisfaction. Jay MacInerney wrote *Bright Lights, Big City* (1984) and *Model Behaviour* (1988). These books cover broadly the same subject matter as Easton Ellis's work. The content of both writers' novels has been compared to F. Scott Fitzgerald.

Dennis Cooper has published four novels: *Frisk* (1992), *Closer* (1994), *Try* (1994) and *Guide* (1998). These books are about degradation of the human spirit and contain scenes of extreme violence. Kathy Acker's *Blood and Guts in High School* (1984) and Douglas Coupland's *Generation X* (1991) also follow in the tradition of William Burroughs.

Tama Janowitz's novels, *Slaves of New York* (1986) and *A Cannibal in Manhattan* (1987), show life in the poorer parts of New York. She has been the first of the brat pack to extend her range of imaginative fiction.

see also...

Cult Fiction

Cold War

This term was coined in the USA after the Second World War. It described the distrust and tension in the economic and political relationship between the power blocks remaining in Europe in 1945. These were the Soviet Bloc (USSR) and the countries of the North Atlantic Treaty Organization (NATO). Despite their common victory over the Axis, the prevailing political ideologies within them led to a situation where they were at war in all but the exchange of bullets. This situation pertained until the 1980s, when political changes in both USSR and USA effectively ended the cold war.

Throughout this period governments employed agents to gather information about the opposing side, thus giving European and American writers the opportunity to produce novels about the cold war. The underlying premise of the genre was that the USSR was engaged in a struggle to take over the western world and that the western world had to maintain eternal vigilance to guard against this. These are novels about espionage and counter-espionage, set in a variety of arenas and triggered by a variety of issues. Yet the conflict is always the same, the fight for supremacy between two opposing ideologies.

Ian Fleming wrote a series of novels in which the spy James Bond was involved in swashbuckling adventures, outwitting the agents of SMERSH. John Le Carre's books adopted a more serious and moralistic stance towards the actions of western agents. In *The Spy Who Came in From the Cold* (1963), he questioned the *carte blanche* approach which governments were said to allow their agents. Len Deighton's *The Ipcress File* (1962) and his later novels raised the same issues. In the USA, Robert Ludlum wrote *The Osterman Weekend* (1972) and *The Matlock Paper* (1973). Both explore the unwilling involvement of individuals who become caught up in cold war conspiracies.

---

see also...

Spies and Secret Agents; Thrillers and Adventures

Comedy and Tragicomedy

Comedy originated in Greece with Aristophanes (450–385 BC). Plays were written for fertility festivals and were satires aimed at named individuals. Many plays were so offensive that they were banned and after 414 BC the old style was replaced by 'new comedy', which relied on broad stereotypes rather than individuals. The style was revived in Italy by Niccolo Machiavelli in *The Mandrake* (1524). The medieval farce developed in Europe as a result of this revival.

During the sixteenth century William Shakespeare wrote *Comedy of Errors* (1594), using complicated plotting, mistaken identity and cross-dressing. Comedies included scenes with stereotypical characters such as clowns. The 'cloak and sword' plays of the Spanish playwright Lope de Vega extended the range and maintained the popularity of comedy. In 1658, Molière started the Comedie Française, solely to perform classical and medieval comedy. A form known as the 'tearful comedy', which included some elements of tragedy in the story, emerged. Voltaire's *L'enfant Prodigue* (1736) is an example. This blend of styles is sometimes called 'tragicomedy'.

Following the Commonwealth and Protectorate period in England, (1649–60) and the restoration of the monarchy, Charles II reopened theatres. Comedy was again revived and was bawdy and dissolute. The plays of William Congreve (*The Way of the World*, 1693); William Wycherly (*The Country Wife*, 1675); and George Farquhar (*The Beaux Stratagem*, 1707), are still performed. In the eighteenth century, playwrights such as Samuel Johnson and Richard Steele extended the range of characters.

Romanticism caused comedy to become less caustic, and two strands emerged. One was light comedy and the other was farce. Farce relied on the traditional form based on satire and parody. These remain the basis of modern comedy.

see also...

Parody; Satire; Tragedy

Concrete Poetry

Concrete poetry developed during the 1950s and 1960s following The National Exhibition of Concrete Art in Sao Paolo, Brazil in 1956. The term 'concrete art' had been introduced in the 1930s by the Dutch painter Theo van Doesburg. It was applied to a form of art which privileged simple geometric shapes, colour and form over naturalistic or figurative representation.

In poetry, the movement was born out of some poets' desire to increase awareness of the physical space which poetry occupies, that is, to treat the visual and technological design of the poem as part of the poem. Since most poetry is read, rather than heard, the typography and other aspects of the graphic design have an impact on the reader's interpretation of the work. Concrete poets used the shape as well as the words to convey meanings.

The ideas of Haroldo do Campos and his brother Augusto were central to the development of concrete poetry. They were instrumental in extending Brazilian awareness of international artistic trends, but their poetry was so complicated that it was seen as elitist by other poets who felt that democratization was more important than theoretical debates about art. This second group, the 'mimeograph' poets, freely copied and distributed their work.

Ian Hamilton Finlay is one of the best known of the concrete poets. He has established a sculpture garden at Stoney path in Scotland where he exhibits work which combines poetry and sculpture with the environment. In this way he 'concretizes' poetry in the physical space which it occupies, which in this case is not the page.

Edwin Morgan has published several collections. His works blend aspects of concrete poetry with more traditional forms and this can be seen in *Glasgow Sonnets* (1952) and *You: Anti-war Poetry* (1991).

see also...

Performance Poetry; Underground Poetry

Crime Fiction

There is a growing body of crime writing in which the narrative is developed from the point of view of the criminal, rather than that of the detective or the victim. Writers often use this perspective to explore the psychological state and motivation of criminals. Some adopt a moral stance and invite readers to do the same, while others seem to accept criminals as simply living an alternative lifestyle and do not judge their characters. Many of the writers who adopt this style have had personal experiences which have allowed them close observation of criminal fraternities.

Patrick Hamilton's play about two young men who murder their friend only for the thrill of committing the crime, *Rope* (1929), is an example of this style. The play was filmed in 1948 and was directed by Alfred Hitchcock.

Laurence Block wrote a series of novels in which the main character is the burglar, Bernie Rhodenbarr. These were similar in atmosphere to an earlier series of books by the English writer Ernest Hornung, who created a 'gentleman thief' named Raffles. Raffles's first appearance was in *The Amateur Cracksman* (1899).

Jim Thompson wrote about gangsters in America. His best-known novel is *The Grifters* (1963). Mario Puzo wrote *The Godfather* (1969), which tells the story of a family of criminals. Emmett Grogan's novel *Final Score* (1978) allows some of the main protagonists to avoid detection.

The novels of James Ellroy are set in Los Angeles, and his life experiences and interest in unsolved murders and police corruption have influenced his choice of material in *The Black Dahlia* (1987) and *American Tabloid* (1995). Elmore Leonard, author of *Get Shorty* (1990), represents the police as flawed and the criminals as opportunists. Jake Arnott wrote *The Long Firm* (1999) which tells the story of British gangsters in the 1960s.

see also...

Detective Fiction

Cult Fiction

Culture is defined as the development of mind, body and spirit by training and experience. This word is used to describe intellectual development in society and individuals and particular forms of such development. Thus we may speak of national cultures, or say that a person is 'cultured'. Sometimes individual behaviour is described as 'cultural', by which the speaker implies that person is behaving typically or stereotypically. An additional meaning is to grow or cultivate. The conceptual link with human development is clear.

In Europe, the idea of culture carries within it a hierarchy, which distinguishes between 'high' and 'low' culture. Traditionally, some art forms and texts have been regarded as 'high', for example, Opera, while others, such as television and detective stories, have been regarded as 'low'. In this hierarchy, cult and counter cultural writing is usually regarded as 'low'.

A cult is practised by fewer people than a culture. It is usually defined only in religious terms as a system of beliefs and worship which includes devotion to an individual or a set of practices. Cults operate on the margins and extremes of mainstream cultures. A sub-cult involves an even smaller number of people. Counter cultural writing offers a direct challenge to mainstream social practices.

Thus, 'cult fiction' is a term applied to non-mainstream texts and writers who have a small, yet dedicated, group of readers. Novels are often about deviant social behaviour or transgression of social and cultural rules, and offer a new philosophy to readers, allowing them to identify with the social dislocation described. Chief characters are sometimes described as 'anti-heroes' rather than heroes. Fans may iconize the writers or regard them with an almost religious fervour, expecting them to be dislocated from the mainstream themselves.

see also...

Beat Generation; Punk and Cyberpunk

Dadaism

The name of this group of writers and artists, which means 'hobby horse', was chosen at random from a dictionary at the inaugural meeting at the Cabaret Voltaire, Zurich, in 1916. Among those present were the German poets Hugo Ball and Hans Arp and the Rumanian poets Marcel Janco and Tristan Tzara. Groups were founded in France, Spain and New York.

Dada was unlike other movements inasmuch as its manifestos did not set out clear outlines of a preferred style and content, but promoted a state of mind. Conceived during the First World War, much of Dadaism was a reaction to the political and social structures which Dadaists believed had caused the War. They were disgusted with the conduct of the War and despaired of a future dominated by the pre-war bourgeoisie. Dadaists preached spontaneity, indifference, cynicism, irrationality and incoherence. They were seen as being both anarchic and nihilistic.

In 1917 many Dadaists moved to Paris, including the poets Louis Aragon, Paul Eluarde and André Breton and the artist Marcel Duchamp. Publication of the magazine, *Litterature,* later renamed *Dada,* began in 1919, edited by Aragon. A group began in Berlin and in New York, Alfred Stieglitz continued the centre based at the Gallery 291 with the photographer Man Ray. The magazine *391* was edited by Francis Picabia.

In 1918, Tzara published the *Dada Manifesto.* It explained that writing is the product of a writer's necessity to write, but that Dada was useless. He wrote a *Chronicle* of Zurich Dada (1922). In Cologne in 1920, an exhibition was closed down as obscene. In 1922, an exhibition by Modigliani, Kandinsky, Klee and Ernst and the poets Kurt Schwitters and Anna Blume was held in Paris.

Dadaists left the group as surrealism challenged Dada's outlook. Aspects of both were later incorporated into the Lettrists and Situationists.

see also...

Nihilism; Surrealism

Decadence

Decadence can be defined as an attitude adopted by people at a time when moral and spiritual exhaustion causes them to question, or even ignore, accepted values, social customs, and moral certainties. Members of society publicly reject and transgress the social rules, which they have previously upheld, and pursue personal physical and sensual pleasure instead. Those who pretend to accept traditional values, but who are insincere and continually transgress society's rules, can also be described as decadent.

Philosophers and historians have often represented decadence as part of a natural cycle, which operates within developed societies and cultures. The fall of the Roman Empire, and America in the 1920s, are often cited as evidence. A more modern view is that decadence is intermittent aberrant behaviour which emerges when governments and societies become dysfunctional and cannot provide what people need or want. They therefore lose the support of individuals.

Literary decadence was first associated with the French symbolist writers of the nineteenth century. The writers of the post-romantic period were criticized for their perverse taste, unconventional behaviour, and their tendency to be obsessively self-expressive. *Against The Grain* (1884), by Joris-Karl Huysmans, abandoned naturalism and substituted sensuousness.

The works of Oscar Wilde are sometimes seen as decadent, with the emphasis on Walter Pater's theory of 'art for art's sake' extended to an almost religious commitment to beauty. *Salome* (1894), was refused a licence in England because of its biblical subject. Many of Wilde's works were illustrated by Aubrey Beardsley, who reflected the *fin-de-siecle* decadence which manifested as the nineteenth century became the twentieth.

see also...

Brat Pack; Jazz Age; Punk and Cyberpunk

Detective Fiction

In classic detective fiction, the narrative adheres to a set of conventions which define the genre. Although not all elements are present in every book, the reader may expect to find intricate plots, crimes which pose intellectual puzzles for detectives, a set of clues, attempts by the writer to misdirect the reader's attempts to solve the puzzle, and eventual solution, capture and punishment. The detective, who takes a particular moral position in relation to the crime and the other characters, is usually drawn from the tradition of the 'lonely outsider'.

These conventions were developed through the work of three writers: Edgar Allen Poe created Dupin in the 1840s; Wilkie Collins created Sergeant Cuff in *The Moonstone* (1868); and Sir Arthur Conan Doyle created Sherlock Holmes in *A Study in Scarlet* (1887).

The 1920s are sometimes called the 'Golden Age' of the detective story. Agatha Christie wrote 66 novels featuring two detectives, Hercule Poirot and Miss Marple. Dorothy L. Sayers incorporated comic elements into her detective, Lord Peter Wimsey. Margery Allingham and Ngaio Marsh were also prolific.

Raymond Chandler had Philip Marlowe solve crimes in Los Angeles in *The Big Sleep* (1939) while Dashiell Hammett's Sam Spade solved the case of *The Maltese Falcon* (1930) in New York. James M. Cain used the criminal as narrator in *The Postman Always Rings Twice* (1934). An exceptional detective was Georges Simenon's Maigret, who worked from intuition, not clues.

By the 1950s, readers preferred realism in crime fiction. Patricia Highsmith, P. D. James, Ruth Rendell and Colin Dexter provided it. In the 1990s the emphasis moved towards realistic representations of police departments. The work of Chester Himes, Elmore Leonard and Ian Rankin, reflects this.

see also...

Crime Fiction; Thrillers and Adventures

Diaries

In England there is a tradition of producing the comic diaries of fictional characters. One of the earliest examples was *The Diary of a Nobody* (1892), by George and Weedon Grossmith. In the twentieth century, *The Diary of a Provincial Lady* (1953) by E M. Delafield *The Secret Diary Of Adrian Mole, Aged 13 1/4* (1982) by Sue Townsend; and *Bridget Jones's Diary* (1996) by Helen Fielding were best-sellers. In each case, the recording of the fictional diarist's secret thoughts and opinions have been an opportunity to show how mundane and shallow human existence can be, whilst demonstrating the sustenance gained by wishes, hopes and dreams.

Such fictional diaries refer to the more serious literary traditions of publishing genuine diaries and journals, which in England can be traced back to Samuel Pepys and John Evelyn. The diary of the founder of Methodism, John Wesley, was published in 1909. Throughout the nineteenth and twentieth centuries, literary, artistic and political figures have published their diaries. Political diaries are of enduring popularity and the genre is thriving.

One of the most famous modern diaries is *The Diary of Anne Frank*, published posthumously in 1947. This records a Jewish teenager's life in hiding with her family during the Nazi occupation of Holland in the Second World War. The family were captured and sent to concentration camps, where Anne was murdered.

Late twentieth-century diarists and their editors are less circumspect in the selection of material than earlier writers. Including controversial material, often of a sexual nature, began with the publication of *Diaries* of the playwright Joe Orton in 1986, which contained passages concerning homosexuality. Modern publishing conventions and libel laws have resulted in posthumous publication of the diaries of many public figures.

see also...

Biographical and Autobiographical Writing

Dissidence

To dissent is to disagree, refuse or to withdraw consent. In a political context, dissident thinks differently from and therefore dissents from and opposes mainstream ideas. The word is commonly used to describe writers who express their opposition to the dominant political thinking within the state or country in which they live. It is especially applied to those who dissent from the official line dictated by the governments of totalitarian states. Thus, German writers who opposed Hitler, Russian writers who opposed Stalin's Socialist Realism, South Africans who opposed apartheid and writers in countless other countries have been described as dissident.

It is not in the nature of totalitarianism to tolerate dissidence, especially among writers, who are in a position to spread oppositional ideas. Freedom of speech and expression are suppressed by totalitarian governments, many of which have taken action against writers. Writers continue to challenge government policies and actions from an individual need for freedom, or from a commitment to hastening or reversing social or political change. Action taken by governments has included banning publication, imprisonment, internal exile and deportation. Some writers have avoided government action by escaping, while others have committed suicide. A few writers have been executed for their beliefs.

Participants in political opposition within democracies are rarely described as dissident. Freedom of speech is embedded in democratic freedom. However, democracies also have laws which regulate, control and censor publication, often as part of national security precautions. Such laws are the focus of struggle for writers, for example, those who refused to testify to the House Committee on Un-American Activities in the USA during the 1940s and 1950s.

see also...

Banned, Exiled and Imprisoned Writers; Socialist Realism

Epic Theatre

A form of theatre writing and production developed by Berthold Brecht in Germany from about 1924 onwards. The form takes its name from the *epic,* a style of narrative poetry which celebrates the deeds of actual or fictional heroes. Epics occur in many cultures and include the classical *Iliad* and *Odyssey* attributed to Homer; the Anglo-Saxon *Beowulf,* and the Hindu *Mahabharata* and *Ramayana.* The first epics were part of the literature of oral cultures, the poetic form helping storytellers to remember the tales at gatherings. Later, poets wrote down epics and Virgil's *Aeneid,* Dante's *Inferno*; and John Milton's *Paradise Lost* are examples. The conventions of epic poetry demand formal language to describe serious, earth-shattering events and some involvement of the gods.

After producing his early work in the expressionist mode, Brecht collaborated with Edwin Piscator and used aspects of epic form. Brecht had early success with *The Threepenny Opera* (1928), working with Kurt Weill. Using summaries, songs, few props and acting styles which kept the actors distant from the characters they played, epic theatre encouraged audiences to engage with theatre in a new way. The intention was to create a form which offered audiences a deeper understanding of their own humanity and a sense of their own potential as individuals and members of society. Brecht's plays include *Mother Courage and her Children* (1941) and *The Resistible Rise of Arturo Ui* (1958).

A Marxist, Brecht left Germany after the rise of Hitler. He lived in Europe and the USA between 1933 and 1947 and left the USA after investigation by the House Un-American Activities Committee headed by Senator Joseph McCarthy. Brecht returned to East Germany in 1948 with his wife Helene Weigel and formed the Berliner Ensemble. This company became central to the development of drama in Europe.

see also...

Expressionism

Epistolary Writing

E pistle is the Greek word for letter, and epistolary writing is the name given to an early form of the novel, where the story is written in the form of letters. The events are told in the first person, or persons as the case may be, throughout. This form was popular in the sixteenth and seventeenth centuries, before the use of a third person narrator was developed.

An early example of the epistolary novel is Aphra Behn's *Love Letters Between a Nobleman and his Sister* (1683), which contained risqué subject matter and was partly responsible for the poor reputation suffered by this form.

Samuel Richardson's *Pamela: or Virtue Rewarded* (1740) attempted to make the form respectable again with a tale of a woman defending her virtue against terrible odds. Henry Fielding wrote a pastiche of Richardson's book called *Shamela* (1741), based on Richardson's characters, but with low moral attitudes. Tobias Smollett wrote *The Expedition of Humphrey Clinker* (1771), in which the letters are from seven correspondents, each acting as narrator, and Fanny Burney wrote *Evelina, or a Young Lady's Entrance into the World* (1778).

Jane Austen experimented with the form in her novel *Lady Susan* (1793), and also wrote a short piece called *Elinor and Marianne*, which was her first version of *Sense and Sensibility* (1811). Much later the poet Algernon Charles Swinburne revived the form with *A Year's Letters* (1877), which was republished in 1905 as *Love's Cross Currents*.

In the twentieth century, some writers continued to explore this style. Henry James produced several short stories based on the exchange of letters. Alice Walker's novel *The Colour Purple* (1983) takes the form of a young girl's letters to God. Russell Hoban's *Turtle Diary* and William Golding's novel *Rites of Passage* (1980) are both epistolary.

see also...

Diaries

Essays

The term essay was first used in English by Francis Bacon in *Essays* (1597), although Montaigne had published a collection of writing, *Essais*, in 1580. The word is derived from the Old French *'essayer'* – to weigh, test or attempt. The links with assaying precious metal are clear, and this sense of testing is present in the literary application of the word. Thus, an essay is the testing or weighing of ideas and arguments and inherent in this is a suggestion of balance.

The second edition of Bacon's *Essays* (1610) contained 38 pieces on a variety of subjects, including civil and public life, *Of Great Life*, and the social factors affecting human life, *Of Friendship*. Bacon's model was adopted by others, among them Sir Thomas Browne who wrote *On Dreams*.

In the seventeenth century, Daniel Defoe, Jonathan Swift, Richard Steele and Joseph Addison published classic examples of the form. Addison's series was based on the life of the fictional *Sir Roger de Coverley* and Charles Lamb's *Essays of Elia* (1820) gave advice on manners and morals. Also writing essays at this time were Samuel Johnson and Oliver Goldsmith. William Hazlitt revived and developed essay writing.

Essays remained popular throughout the nineteenth century. Leigh Hunt, Thomas de Quincey and John Ruskin published literary criticism as essays. Matthew Arnold published three volumes entitled *Essays in Criticism* (1865, 1888, and 1910). Ralph Waldo Emerson, used essays to explain his personal philosophy and James Russell Lowell travelled widely in Europe and presented his thoughts to the American public. The form was accessible to women and George Eliot and Mary Coleridge published collections.

Although some essays were published during the twentieth century, their popularity had waned. Susan Sontag's *On Photography* (1977); Gore Vidal's *Matters of Fact and Fiction* (1977); and Alice Walker's *In Search of My Mother's Garden* (1983) are modern examples.

Ethnic Fiction

thnic fiction is the term used to describe writing by members of ethnic groups which are in the minority in the country in which they live. Where the mainstream population of a country is drawn from one, usually the largest, ethnic group, then writing emanating from minority groups can be described as 'ethnic'. This description pertains regardless of whether the minority group is indigenous to the country. The movement of people between countries throughout history, whether from voluntary immigration, enforced migration or colonization has left millions of people living in minority ethnic communities.

In some countries, the original inhabitants are now in the minority. The oldest residents of Australia are the indigenous Aboriginal people, yet it is only recently that writers such as Mudrooroo (*Wild Cat Falling*, 1965) and Sally Morgan (*My Place*, 1987), have gained prominence within the context of the dominant white culture. The work of Paula Gunn Allen and Louise Erdrich (*Love Medicine*, 1985), have re-represented the Native American narrative forms, and raised issues about access to publication.

African American writers such as James Baldwin (*Another Country*, 1962) and Toni Morrison (*Beloved*, 1987) explored the relationship between the dominant white culture and black Americans. Maxine Hong Kingston's *Tripmaster Monkey* (1989) explores the lives of Chinese Americans, while Bernard Malamud and Saul Bellow examined the relationship between Jews and Gentiles. Minority ethnic fiction is not concerned only with cultural and political relationships, and writers produce work in a range of genres regardless of their ethnic backgrounds.

In Britain and Europe, the ethnic mix is a result of colonization and immigration. The works of an increasing number of Black and Asian British writers are now published.

see also...

Post-colonial Literatures

Existentialism

Existentialism is concerned with the philosophy of existence. The philosophers Soron Kierkegaard, Martin Heidegger and Karl Jaspers developed the theory.

Existentialists reject belief in the pre-existing essence of humanity, which is said to motivate our building of qualities, attitudes and expectations within which we live. Human nature is seen instead as an invention by the powerful members of society, as a method of keeping people under control. For existentialists, human nature does not exist, and the constraints of conformity are illusory. It follows that all people are free to make choices. Existentialists see individuals as unique and at the centre of their own world, with total responsibility for their actions and with no need to justify their actions. Free choice is all. Choosing one option from a range automatically excludes all others, and the consequences of choice lie entirely with the individual. Therefore, every individual is merely the sum of his or her own actions. Choices should not be made lightly, as any choice limits future options

unknown when making any given decision. The existentialist position reveals the absurdity of the human condition and the difficulty of creating an honest moral framework for action.

Jean Paul Sartre argued that the moral individual makes choices in 'good faith', that is, fully aware of the consequences and certain that the choice would still be good if everybody made the same choice. Those who act in 'bad faith' try to escape responsibility for their actions and are hypocritical because they claim to act in the interest of others while really acting from self-interest. Sartre explores this in *The Roads to Freedom* (1947–50). Simone de Beauvoir explored feminism from an existential standpoint.

Albert Camus, in *The Plague* (1947); *The Rebel* (1951); and *The Fall* (1956), argued that a moral, not political, revolution was necessary.

see also...

Dadaism; Surrealism; Theatre of the Absurd

Expressionism

Expressionism was a European art movement, which developed in Germany after 1900, although the word was first used by the French painter Julien-Auguste Herve. Expressionists showed what they felt. In the attempt to express their subjective and emotional reactions to the world, artists often used distortion and exaggeration of shape and colour in abstract compositions.

From about 1910 onwards a corresponding movement in literature emphasized the will of the individual and the expression of experience. Writing is characterized by the refusal to recreate or imitate what already exists and is anti-realist in intent and execution. Expressionist writers start from the emotions and allow them to dictate the form of the text. The text is sometimes disjointed, rich in imagery and with a bias towards the visionary. After the First World War, the atmosphere of rebellion against the old political systems, especially in Germany, allowed expressionism to flourish.

The dramatists Georg Kaiser and Ernst Toller used a technique called 'compression'. This omitted all detail except that which contributed directly to the central idea of the play. Characters were presented as if they had no existence outside the text, events external to the play were not referred to, scenes were connected by ideas rather than logical continuity of action. An economic use of language in dialogue, which gives a disjointed and staccato effect, has been compared to the style used in telegrams or text messages. The productions were consonant with expressionist ideas. Lighting and scenery were designed to create a dreamlike, distorted vision.

Expressionist prose writers include Leonhard Frank, Alfred Doblin and Franz Werfel. While almost exclusively a German movement, Wyndham Lewis and Eugene O'Neill experimented with the style.

see also...
Epic Theatre; Gruppe 47

Faction

This term was created in the 1970s to describe a genre of fiction writing which relies heavily on incorporating facts within the body of the text, without identifying them as facts. After the publication of several works which are neither pure fiction nor pure non-fiction, this portfolio word was coined and rapidly accepted into use, first in publishing and later in film and television production.

Truman Capote's *In Cold Blood* was published in 1966, and Capote described his work as a 'non-fiction novel'. It tells the story of two murderers who had been executed in 1965, and reconstructs the lives of everybody who had been involved in the crime. His thorough research and documentary or journalistic style allowed him to link facts with fictional episodes, thus creating a new genre.

In Norman Mailer's *Armies of the Night* (1969), which won the Pulitzer Prize, he used this technique to write about the USA's involvement in the Vietnam War of 1964–75. Mailer won a second Pullitzer Prize in 1980 for his book

The Executioner's Song (1980).

In America, the work of Capote and Mailer influenced journalism as well as fiction. A style known as 'new journalism' evolved in the 1970s. Key figures in this movement were Tom Wolfe (*The Electric Kool-Aid Acid Test*, 1968), and Hunter S. Thompson who wrote a scathing account of the 1972 Democratic Party Convention in *Fear and Loathing in Las Vegas* (1972).

Thomas Keneally wrote about a German factory owner who became involved in saving Jews who worked for him in Nazi occupied Poland from the gas chambers. This book has the distinction of having been published as both fiction and non-fiction. As *Schindler's Ark* (1982) it was published in Britain and Australia as fiction, while in the USA it was published as non-fiction as *Schindler's List*.

see also...
Graphic Novel

Fantasy Fiction

The events in fantasy fiction usually occur in unstated or indeterminate locations, at any time. The writing offers readers freedom from the constraints of reality and creates societies whose internal rules are coherent and logical. Writers can address topics which are outside the range of the traditional novel.

Lewis Carroll created a fantasy world in *Alice's Adventures in Wonderland* (1865). Lord Dunsany wrote stories, poems and novels including *The King of Elfland's Daughter* (1924).

During the twentieth century, E. R. Eddison (*The Worm Ourobouros*, 1922) and Mervyn Peake (*Gormenghast Trilogy*, 1946–59) created memorable worlds. J. R. R. Tolkien wrote *The Hobbit* (1937) and *The Lord of the Rings* (1954–6). Tolkien created a detailed world, including language. Stephen Donaldson's *Chronicles of Thomas Covenant* (1977) is concerned with ecological issues. In Michael Moorcock's *The Sundered Worlds* (1965), the hero inhabits a multiverse with different layers of reality and changes characters throughout. Russell Hoban reinvents our own times in *Riddley Walker* (1980).

In the USA, there is a tradition of magazine publication. H. P. Lovecraft's stories and Robert E. Howard's imaginary mythology, *Conan the Barbarian* were published in this form. Robert Heinlein relates scientific development to imaginary cultures where scientists become magicians. Anne McCaffrey in *Dragonflight* (1968) and Ursula Le Guin with *The Dispossessed* (1974), have created fantasy worlds.

Comic fantasy such as Douglas Adams's *The Hitchhiker's Guide to the Galaxy* (1979) is very popular. Terry Pratchett's *The Colour of Magic* (1983) was the first in the series about Discworld. Children's fantasy includes Philip Pullman's trilogy, *His Dark Materials*, and J. K. Rowling's books about Harry Potter.

see also...

Magical Realism; Science Fiction; Utopias

Feminist Writing

Feminist writing first appeared in Europe during the Enlightenment. Writers, philosophers and politicians began to address the implications of social organization based on inherited privilege. Modern ideas suggested that a continuation of societies modelled on the feudal system was no longer appropriate and that a more equitable arrangement should be adopted.

In England, Thomas Paine, William Godwin and William Blake dissented from the status quo, and in France, Jean Jacques Rousseau's *The Social Contract* (1762) exhorted change. Women were determined that female oppression, based on assumptions of male superiority over women, should be eradicated. Women joined dissenting and revolutionary groups. Mary Wollstonecraft's *A Vindication of the Rights of Women* (1792) claimed that femininity was a male construct whose purpose was the continuance of the male power base.

In France, two revolutionary factions, the Jacobins, and the Girondins, embraced aspects of feminism. The Girondin, Olympe de Gouge published the *Declaration of the Rights of Women* (1791). In America, Lucy Stone and in Russia, Alexandra Kollontai campaigned for social and political change.

During the nineteenth century, much feminist work was published. All feminist writing is radical because the intention is to upset the status quo, yet all writing by women is not feminist. Literary traditions are now established in political manifestos, social and cultural analysis, literary criticism, biography, autobiography and all forms of fiction. A particular feature of feminism has been the republication of neglected women writers.

In the twentieth century, feminists continued to fight for equality. Buchi Emecheta, Margaret Atwood, Alice Walker and Maxine Hong Kingston describe the conditions of women's lives.

see also...

Gay and Lesbian Literature

Formalism and New Criticism

Formalism was an approach to literary criticism developed in Russia during the late nineteenth century. Roman Jakobson and Victor Shklovsky introduced a scientific method of criticism which concentrated on writers' use of language, linguistic 'devices' and conventions. They believed that these things separate literature from other uses of language and that by studying the techniques used by writers, objective criticism could be developed. The adoption of such a formal approach meant that form and style became more important than content and that all information about the writer, and all political and moral content was seen as extraneous. Formalism was developed in opposition to traditional schools of criticism, which also considered content and perceived moral value of texts.

After Stalin came to power in Russia, the policy of Socialist Realism returned the emphasis to content. In 1926, Jakobson moved to Prague, where he founded the Prague Linguistic Circle. This group influenced linguists and philosophers, some of whom became structuralists.

In England, I. A. Richards had written *The Meaning of Meaning* (1924) and *Practical Criticism* (1929). William Empson (*Poems*, 1905 and *Seven Types of Ambiguity*, 1930) embraced a more formal approach to literature and was interested in basic use of English and the exact meanings of words.

By the 1930s, the ideas of the formalists had reached the USA, and 'New Criticism' was born. Cleanth Brooks and Robert Penn Warren co-edited a literary magazine, the *Southern Review*, between 1935 and 1942. They rejected what they called the 'extrinsic' approach to poetry and thought criticism and analysis should concentrate only on what was 'on the page'. Brooks and Penn Warren expounded this view in *Understanding Poetry* (1938). Brooks developed the ideas in *The Well Wrought Urn* (1947).

see also...

Socialist Realism; Structuralism and Post-structuralism

Free Verse

Free verse challenges the conventions of traditional poetic structures. Poetry is based on arranging syllables and words into regularly recurring and predictable stress patterns. A line of words is measured in metric feet, by the number of stresses. In free verse these rhythms are broken up by using the 'variable foot', to give lines of different lengths. The poet has more freedom to make irregular sound patterns than within the standard patterns of the metric foot. Free verse is also characterized by the repetition of phrases and irregular rhyme patterns. This irregularity in metric feet and end rhyme can be heard and seen in print.

Free verse has been described as a more democratic form of poetry than traditional forms which demand more formality. Many poets have composed free verse using colloquial and idiomatic language.

Johann Wolfgang von Goethe experimented with non-traditional forms, but two poets are best known for popularizing free verse,

Walt Whitman (*Leaves of Grass*, 1855) and Arthur Rimbaud (*Illuminations*, 1873).

During the twentieth century, the most significant influence on the development of free verse was from the Imagist poets. This can be seen in the work of Guillame Appolinaire and the Symbolist poet Rainer Maria Rilke with *Life and Songs* (1894) and *Sonnets to Orpheus* (1923). Gabriel d'Annuncio also experimented with this form.

T. S. Eliot, Ezra Pound and William Carlos Williams also used this form. Williams wrote *Paterson* (1946–58), in what he called 'the American idiom' and influenced Allen Ginsberg and Robert Lowell. e. e. cummings extended the form. He moved line breaks away, causing an effect of syncopation, and used only lower case letters in *50 Poems* (1940) and *95 Poems* (1958).

see also...

Imagism; Performance Poetry; Symbolism; Underground Poetry

Fringe

A fringe is on the edge of something else, in the way that 'fringe benefits' are additional to the actual salary for a job. Fringe events are organized around mainstream events, for example, literature and arts festivals may have 'fringe festivals' operating concurrently. The rationale behind fringe events is to increase the range of the core events, to attract different and new audiences and to showcase work by writers and artists whose work is not well known. Fringe events occur in relation to 'official' events, for it is the mainstream events which give a context to the concept. Originally fringe festivals were organized after the main events, but many festivals now have fringe organizers who work in a proactive rather than a reactive way. The most famous example of this is the Edinburgh International Festival in Scotland, where the Edinburgh Fringe Festival runs thousands of events during the 'official' festival.

Closely allied to the fringe is the 'margin'. The work of many writers can be described as fringe, marginal, or even as marginalized from the mainstream. Writers who depend on publishers, and playwrights who depend on theatres, rely on commercial mainstream institutions to publish or perform texts. Arts businesses must trade at a profit like other organizations, and if they are unconvinced that investment will be recouped, a text is unlikely to be published. Many writers and performers who operate on the fringe or margin of mainstream organizations could legitimately claim to have been marginalized by them. There is a sense of purposeful exclusion in this concept.

The content and form of fringe writing varies with the social and political climate of the country involved. For example, in England before 1969, it was illegal to publish material containing direct references to homosexuality. With changes in the law, gay and lesbian literature is now part of mainstream publishing.

see also...

Epic Theatre; Feminist Writing; Performance Poetry

35

Futurism

Futurism was a European movement of the arts in the early twentieth century. *The Founding and Manifesto of Futurism* (1909) was published by Filippo Marinetti. The movement challenged every aspect of the past including the conventions of and academic approaches to literature. Futurists exhorted writers and artists to celebrate 'the new' and to abandon the attitudes and values of the past. Writing was to celebrate science, technology and machines, which created dynamism, speed, power and spontaneity in life. Marinetti's vision of the 'free word' demanded that syntax, metre, punctuation, design and typography be destroyed.

New forms arose, including Variety Theatre in 1913, and Synthetic Theatre in 1915. Experimental short dramas reflected the dynamic and abstract values of the movement. Plays cast people as robot-like beings, and designers and painters became increasingly important. In 1924 the Italian Futurists allied to the fascist leader Benito Mussolini, and an anthology, *New Futurist Poems* (1925), was published.

In Russia, left-wing poets called 'men of the future' wrote poetry similar to that of the Futurists. They are called cubo-futurist, due to their interest in using language to produce new meanings and interpretations of the world. They emphasized the sound and texture of words, using dissonant or staccato sounding language and colloquial speech. This was described as 'creative deformation' of language. Velimir Khlebnikov and Vladimir Mayakovsky dominated Russian literature in the 1920s.

Mayakovsky was a member of the Left Front for the Arts. His work *A Cloud in Trousers* (1914–15) was about love, and *Mystery Bouffe* (1918) was a milestone of the revolution. In 1923, Stalin's government disbanded the Left Front. Mayakovsky's later plays were banned. He committed suicide in 1930.

see also...

Modernism; Socialist Realism

Gay and Lesbian Literature

Gay, lesbian and bisexual literature can be defined in two ways. Firstly, texts produced by writers who are themselves members of these groups, and secondly, works by heterosexuals which are supportive of those who are not. Throughout history, heterosexuality has been represented by ruling groups in all societies as the only acceptable way to express love. The history of gay, lesbian and bisexual writing is also the history of the power struggle for publication, and against censorship, suppression and, in some cases, imprisonment.

Plato's *Symposium*, Ovid's *Metamorphoses* and the poems of Sappho are among the earliest examples of writing which address the issues of love and sexuality. Both Edmund Spenser's *Shepherde's Calendar* (1579) and William Shakespeare's *Sonnets* contained homo-erotic sections.

In the nineteenth century, more gay and lesbian fiction was published, although works were often disguised by allegory. In England, Edward Carpenter's poem *Towards Democracy* (1883–1902), and in the USA, Sarah Orne Jewett's *The Country of the Pointed Firs* (1896), broke new ground. However, Oscar Wilde's *De Profundis* was unpublished until 1905 and E. M. Forster's *Maurice* (1913) was suppressed until 1972. Radclyffe Hall's *The Well of Loneliness* (1928) was published, but was banned after a trial for obscenity.

By the end of the twentieth century it was possible for gay, lesbian and bisexual writers to publish their work in most western countries. The political and cultural changes forced by organizations such as the Gay Liberation Front and groups within the women's movement resulted in liberalization of the laws governing homo-sexuality and obscenity. Today, gay, lesbian and bisexual writers publish work across a range of genres, for example, Jeannette Winterson's *Oranges Are Not the Only Fruit* (1985) and Adam Mars Jones's *The Waters of Thirst* (1993).

see also...

Feminist Writing

37

Genre

Genre is a French word, which translates into English as: type, sort, kind, genus, family or style. Genre theory suggests that fiction which shares content, style and conventions can be sorted into categories or genres.

Two assumptions are made. First, that it is possible to decide definitively which book belongs in which category, and second, that every book can be allocated to one genre or another. This appears to be a simple process and one by which anybody can assign a given book to a category. In some cases this is true. For example, all books written by Agatha Christie can easily be placed within the genre 'detective stories'. Umberto Eco's *The Name of the Rose* (1980), while obviously using the conventions of a 'detective story', is set in a medieval Italian monastery and therefore includes many elements which could reasonably allow it to be categorized as 'historical novel' or 'magical realism'. The characters in Eco's novel also discuss language, truth and philosophy, and especially semiotics, the science of how signs are used to create meanings. This excludes the novel from all the other categories to which it could be assigned, and could lead the reader to imagine a genre, or perhaps a sub-genre, called 'semiotic novels'.

There are no hard and fast rules about genre, or about how many different genres and sub-genres exist, although the use of certain conventions may indicate that a work falls more into one genre than another. Writers may decide to write within a genre, literary critics and scholars may try to assign books to certain genres, booksellers or librarians may display books in genre sections, or readers themselves may think of a certain book as being within one genre or another. Some genres, for example, tragedy and romance, are as old as written literature itself. New genres, such as cyberpunk are still being created, as writers find new things to write about and push back the boundaries of form and convention.

Georgian Poets

The Georgian Poets, unlike other groups, did not come together because of shared beliefs or intentions, but because the poets Rupert Brooke, Harold Monro and Edward Marsh embarked on a publishing venture in England in 1912. They published verse and poetry by young British poets, and named the anthologies they printed after the new King, George V, who had succeeded to the throne in 1910. Five anthologies were published on a biennial basis between 1912 and 1922, and for the most part the content was Victorian in its sentimental outlook.

The rural idylls portrayed by John Masefield in *The Everlasting Mercy* and A. E. Housman's *The Shropshire Ballads* were the touchstones of the Georgian venture. Early works by a number of poets were included. W. H. Davies (*Complete Poems*, 1963); Walter de la Mare (*The Listeners*, 1912); Lascelles Abercrombie (*Collected Poems*, 1930); and Ralph Hodgson (*Collected Poems*, 1961) were major contributors to the series and went on to publish work in other literary forms. Some poets did not retain the Georgian atmosphere of their earlier work. The lesser-known poets Frances Brett Young, Gordon Bottomley and John Drinkwater did not consolidate their early success.

Of the young Georgian poets who served in the First World War, three were killed in action: Rupert Brooke ((*1914 and Other Poems*, 1915), Isaac Rosenberg (*Collected Works*, 1937), and Edward Thomas (*Collected Poems*, 1978).

Other members of the group found themselves so affected by the experience of war that they abandoned their pre-war idealism and wrote with a greater degree of realism. These included Robert Graves (*Collected Poems*, 1975); Siegfried Sassoon (*Collected Poems*, 1957); Edmund Blunden (*Collected Poems*, 1930); and Wilfred Wilson Gibson (*Collected Poems 1905–1925*, published in 1926).

see also...

Victorian Literature; War Poetry

Ghost Stories

This genre is a relatively modern literary development. During the Victorian era, the power of the dead to return and confront the living became of interest to readers and writers, and the genre flourished. Against the nineteenth-century background of continual rational scientific and industrial development, a desire to read about the spiritual and inexplicable was identified and met.

Ghosts in Victorian stories inhabited their own moral and physical universe, but were driven to return to the living world. In earlier literature, ghosts had returned for a specific purpose, usually to make prophecies or to impart information. They did arouse fear when they manifested, but this was transient, and ghosts were less important than their messages. Victorian writers introduced malevolent ghosts who sometimes failed to manifest physically, but insinuated themselves directly into the human mind or took control of objects. This reflects widespread public interest in spiritualism.

Whereas Gothic writers had placed ghosts in unreal and imaginary situations, modern ghosts intervene directly in ordinary situations. This allows the writer to exploit the inherent suspense and fear in the tale. This occurs in Walter Scott's *The Tapestried Chamber* (1828), the stories of J. Sheridan le Fanu and Charles Dickens's *The Signalman* (1866). Henry James's *The Turn of the Screw* (1898) is one of the most famous ghost stories ever written.

Ghost stories were popular among women writers. Mary Elizabeth Braddon, Rhoda Broughton and Edith Wharton (*Tales of Men and Ghosts*, 1910), all wrote within the genre.

Specialist writers include Algernon Blackwood (*The Empty House*, 1906), W.F. Harvey, E.F. Benson and M.R. James. Modern writers include A.N.L. Mumby (*The Alabaster Hand*, 1949) and Susan Hill (*The Woman in Black*, 1983).

see also...

Gothic Fiction; Horror

Gothic Fiction

Gothic tales were originally set in medieval times, which were thought of as having been barbaric times when those with social power did not hesitate to wield it cruelly over the peasants. The books sometimes had a strong anti-Catholic element and usually included elements of horror, violence and the supernatural.

Early examples of Gothic novels, which explore the relationship between what is portrayed as modern enlightenment and the oppression of past times, are *The Castle of Otranto* (1764) by Horace Walpole and *The Mysteries of Udolpho* (1794) by Ann Radcliffe. These feature an innocent and unsuspecting hero or heroine who is trapped and imprisoned by a villainous aristocrat. The setting is often a castle, monastery, or haunted building where sinister and unexplained events take place.

During the nineteenth century, medieval settings were replaced by more modern or contemporary settings. This can be seen in Mary Shelley's *Frankenstein* (1818) where a scientist creates a monster, and also in Edgar Allen Poe's *Fall of the House of Usher* (1839). *Villette* (1853) by Charlotte Brontë, and *Great Expectations* (1860) by Charles Dickens have strong Gothic elements in characterization, story and setting. The classic story of the vampire who visits England, *Dracula* (1897) by Bram Stoker, and Henry James's haunting *The Turn of the Screw* (1898,) kept the Gothic tradition alive.

There was a reworking of Gothic literature during the twentieth century. Many books had their roots in the tradition, of which William Faulkner's *Sanctuary* (1931) and *Absalom, Absalom!* (1936) are examples. Daphne du Maurier's *Rebecca* (1938) revisited the trapped heroine of earlier times. In the 1980s, Angela Carter and Toni Morrison were writing feminist novels which explored contemporary debates about issues in race, sex and gender by reworking Gothic themes.

see also...

Ghost Stories; Horror

Graphic Novel

Pictures pre-date writing and the earliest written communication was in images. Sequences can be found in pre-Columbian art and the Bayeaux Tapestry. Egyptian hieroglyphics represent sounds and thus are not pictorial in the same sense.

In the modern graphic novel, a story is told wholly or mostly in pictures. Comics and graphic novels differ in content and intent and they should not be seen as the same simply because they share methods of production. Graphic novels are written within genres in the same way as other novels. Sequential images are used in comics, graphic novels, film and animation and frames are deliberately ordered. In film and animation, each picture occupies the same space as the previous one, while in a book the frames are static and juxtaposed on the pages.

A number of full-length graphic novels featuring super heroes do have their origins in comics. Examples include the *Batman* and the *Judge Dredd AD 2000* series.

Many graphic novels are written within the horror, magic, fantasy and science fiction genres. Some series are based on television characters and are also examples of novelization. An example is *Ring of Fire* (2000) written by Doug Petrie and illustrated by Ryan Sook taken from *Buffy the Vampire Slayer*.

There has been parallel development of graphic novels in social, political and historical fiction. Art Spiegelman's *Maus, A Survivor's Tale* (1986) in two volumes is about the Holocaust. Enki Bilal and Christin's work revisits political events of the twentieth century in *The Hunting Party* (1990). Alan Moore's *From Hell* (2000) is about Jack the Ripper and Iain Sinclair's *Slow Chocolate Autopsy* (1998) addresses events from the history of London. Will Eisner's *The Building* (1998) is a social satire, as are David Whiteland's *Book of Pages* (2000) and Neil Gaiman's *American Gods* (2000), illustrated by Michael Zulli.

Gruppe 47

Gruppe 47 was started in West Germany after the Second World War under the influence of Hans Werner Richter who edited the left wing newspaper *Der Ruf*. Writers wanted German literature to reflect the changing attitudes of a country wrestling with defeat and guilt. It was hoped that a renaissance in the arts, using language in new ways, could support the reconstruction. Although not overtly political, Gruppe 47 was on the left, and those felt to be right wing, or using the rhetoric, imagery and sentimentality which had fuelled the rise of Hitler, were excluded.

Even language was changing and Gruppe 47 made use of the 'cleaning up' of German. Their radio plays, or horspiel, adopted a documentary drama style. Horspiel were characterized by the use of a successive, rather than progressive structure, allowing the presentation of simultaneous events and were written by expressionist and post-expressionist writers.

Heinrich Boll had been a soldier and a prisoner of war. He became critical of a post-war German society which seemed complacent and explored this in his early novels. In *The Lost Honour of Katharina Blum* (1974), Boll criticized denial, lack of morality and money chasing and considered man's realization of the inability to change destiny and the feelings of desolation which realization induces. The novel was written as a police report and used a conventional realist structure with flashback and interior monologue. The writer's strong anti-war stance was attacked from all sides.

Peter Weiss's play *Marat/Sade* (1964) was inspired by Brecht, and explored the tension between imagination and action. Alfred Andersch's *Flight to Afar* (1958) explored post-war moral values. Gunter Grass wrote partly satirical novels about the pretence that Hitlerism had been merely a youthful phase. *The Tin Drum* (1959) examines this idea.

see also...

Expressionism

Historical Fiction

istorical fiction emerged during the eighteenth century. Horace Walpole's gothic novel *The Castle of Otranto* (1764) is among the first of the genre. By the 1780s it was common for romance stories to be set in the past, whereas serious novels were set in the present, and many of the former were influenced by the Gothic tradition. *Castle Rackrent* (1800), by Maria Edgeworth, is an example of the Gothic historical romance.

In the nineteenth century, two strands emerged. Some novelists produced 'national tales', which created a mythical and romantic past wherein the roots of national culture were located. *The Old English Baron* (1778) by Clara Reeve is an early example and Sir Walter Scott's *Waverley Novels*, a sequence of 25 tales, are within this sub-genre. Similar sub-genres existed in other European countries. This strand survived, with a less nationalistic flavour, in the Regency romances of Georgette Heyer and the novels of Barbara Cartland.

The second strand located serious novels in a well-researched historical background. In 1831, Victor Hugo wrote *Notre Dame de Paris*, set in medieval times. W.M. Thackeray's *The History of Henry Esmonde* (1852), set during the reign of Queen Anne, and George Eliot's *Romola* (1863), set in fifteenth century Florence followed. Charles Reade, Charles Kingsley and Robert Louis Stevenson also wrote within this genre.

A series by C.S. Forester set in the Napoleonic wars, featuring *Horatio Hornblower* and George MacDonald Fraser's *Flashman* series are best-sellers. Mary Renault's novels set in Ancient Greece, and Robert Graves's novels about the Roman Emperors, (*I, Claudius*, 1934) remain popular. Ellis Peters wrote historical detective stories.

More recently, John Fowles's *The French Lieutenant's Woman* (1969); A.S. Byatt's *Possession* (1990); and Barry Unsworth's *Sacred Hunger* (1992) have revived interest in the genre.

see also...

Romantic Fiction

Holocaust

When Adolph Hitler's National Socialist Party (Nazi) came to power in Germany in 1933, the destruction of Judaism was among its policies. As Germany invaded countries, Jews were put into slave labour and concentration camps. By 1942, plans were made for the 'final solution'. This was to be the imprisonment and extermination of all Jews. By 1945, Hitler had killed more than six million Jews. Other victims were Gypsies, homosexuals, political opponents and trade unionists. The time is well documented – letters, diaries and personal accounts are available, as are non-fiction books. There has been a limited amount of fiction, or fictionalized autobiography produced, perhaps because the subject has not seemed appropriate while Holocaust survivors are still alive.

Contemporary poets wrote about what was happening in Europe. Some, like the Romanian Paul Celan, from personal experience of the camps, and others, for example, the American Randall Jarrell, as a soldier. Primo Levi, who survived Auschwitz, saw his work, which includes *If This Is a Man* (1961), as testimony. Sylvia Plath was among the first poets to write about the Holocaust without having witnessed it.

A few novels were written during the late-twentieth century, including *The Last of the Just* (1960) by André Schwarz-Bart and *Blood from the Sky* (1964) by Piotr Rawicz, the story of a family in hiding in the Ukraine.

Later it seemed imperative to write for a new generation of readers. *Sophie's Choice* (1979) by William Styron; *Schindler's Ark* (1982) by Thomas Keneally; and D. M. Thomas's *The White Hotel* (1981) were best-sellers. More recently, Louis Begley's *Wartime Lies* (1991) and Anne Michael's *Fugitive Pieces* (1996) have had a similar impact. Alexander Ramati's *And The Violins Stopped Playing* (1989) is about Romany Gypsies in the Holocaust, while Martin Sherman's play, *Bent* (1979), addresses the persecution of homosexuals.

Horror

The horror genre is a relatively modern development with roots in the Gothic tradition and Romanticism. Both movements emphasized the evocation of emotional responses in the reader. The horror writer also seeks to create psychological and physical responses. The skill lies in creating and maintaining an atmosphere of tension and of sustaining two levels of reality within the story. Reader perception of what is horrifying changes in relation to society's scientific and cultural development, and writers use the power of suggestion to maintain readers' responses.

Sub-genres of horror writing are the supernatural (including ghosts, witches, and vampires), tales which induce physical horror and demonization. Demonization relies on writers' and readers' shared Christian traditions and an acceptance of the co-existence of good and evil. Exotic places, strange artefacts and unknown religious cults are usually included. Science and mysticism are vital components of terror and are balanced to send characters, and sometimes readers, 'over the edge'.

Edgar Allan Poe introduced physical horror. Characters are self-destructive, alienated and suffer their worst nightmares such as being buried alive. For Poe's victims, the evil that befalls them is often the evil carried within themselves. Classic nineteenth-century horror writers include J. Sheridan le Fanu, H.P. Lovecraft and Ambrose Bierce. Robert Louis Stevenson's *The Strange Case of Dr Jekyll and Mr Hyde* (1886) explores the duality within one man.

Modern writers rely on a knowledge of psychology. Stephen King's supernatural horror, *The Shining* (1977), James Herbert's physical horror and Shirley Jackson's blend of both enjoy popularity. Other writers include Clive Barker, Dean R. Kootz, Anne Rice and Muriel Gray.

see also...

Ghost Stories; Gothic Fiction

Imagery

Imagery is a collective term used to describe the devices which writers use to evoke pictures and associations in the mind of the reader. While some critics would wish to limit the concept to refer only to visual images, there is a body of literary theory which has extended the definition to include anything which helps to recreate any experience in any way. Some critics and theorists also include direct description in their definition of imagery. The thinking behind this is that all literature exists to create images in the reader's mind, and therefore anything which achieves this by appealing to the senses is imagery. However, the most common type of image remains visual.

Imagery includes the simile, which is used to liken or compare one thing to another, for example, 'he howled like a dog'. Metaphor extends this concept by suggesting that the qualities of one object can be transferred to another, not necessarily appropriate, object. There is a feeling of compressing ideas and carrying intrinsic qualities across from one object to another, for example, 'the wind howled.'

Metaphors are classified as dead, dying or living. A dead metaphor is one which has lost the power to evoke a response because the original comparison is archaic. For example, the phrase 'money for old rope' has lost its comparative meaning since the trade of salvaging and re-selling ships' ropes has ceased. Dying metaphors are, similarly, archaic in their allusions, yet are still in regular use despite their lack of power. An example of a dying metaphor is, 'putting a shoulder to the wheel'. These are sometimes called clichés. Living metaphors are fresh, vivid, powerful and evocative.

Two more devices are allied. The synedoche allows one part of an object to stand in the place of the whole, for example, the description of workers as 'hands'. The second is metonymy, which allows an object to be described wholly in terms of another, for example, 'the crown' used when referring to a monarch, suggests the indivisibility of the object from the person.

see also...

Metaphysical; Symbolism

Imagism

The imagists were English and American poets writing before the First World War. Their work was born out of a reaction to what they saw as the abstract nature and self-indulgence of nineteenth-century romanticism. The group was influenced by the philosopher and writer Thomas Hulme. Hulme foresaw the rejection of romanticism in both art and writing and a movement towards more economic, geometric forms.

An anthology, *Des Imagistes*, was published in 1914 and edited by Ezra Pound. It included work by William Carlos Williams, Amy Lowell, James Joyce and Hilda Doolittle. Although not part of the original group, some of D.H. Lawrence's work is imagist in structure. The group also published three anthologies edited by Amy Lowell and each entitled *Some Imagist Poets* (1915–17).

The poems are characteristically short and often comprised of only a single image or metaphor. The lines are short and have strong rhythmic patterns. The emphasis was on the clarity and concreteness of the image itself, not on any abstract or symbolic meanings that can be attributed to images. The imagists chose language which allowed as pure and objective a representation of an object or scene as possible. They felt that only in this way could the poetry have the desired and immediate effect of giving readers a new insight into the world. Economy of language and strict adherence to the principles meant that imagists developed an almost scientific approach to poetry.

Imagist poems are often associated with the Japanese lyric style, the Haiku, in which a single thought or image is expressed within the traditional seventeen syllable structure. However, the intention behind the writing of Haiku is quite different.

The movement was short lived, but influenced later poets such as T.S. Eliot and the Russian Sergei Esenin.

see also...

Modernism

Impressionism

Impressionism originated among painters in Paris in the 1860s. Claude Monet, Auguste Renoir and Alfred Sisley held the first of eight exhibitions of impressionist painting in 1874. They painted their impressions of their direct observations of nature, and used only the colours of the spectrum. Their work was representational, not symbolic. The artists particularly tried to capture how light and its refractions constantly changes what we see and how we see it, and tried to reproduce our fleeting impressions of the world. In this, the impressionists were linked to both naturalism and realism, and opposed to romanticism, which was more interested in emotional responses and imaginative subjects.

In Germany, writers were inspired by the impressionists to experiment with the idea of capturing the passing impression of a moment. Their work was closely allied to naturalism, but rejected the attempted objectivity of naturalism in favour of subjectivity. However, the literary movements of realism, naturalism and impressionism shared a desire to use precise language in order to record experiences accurately.

Literary impressionism began with lyric poets. Richard Dehmel's *Weib und Welt* (1896) and the early work of the poet Rainer Maria Rilke, were influential.

The novelist Theodore Fontane wrote *Effi Brest* (1895) and Thomas Mann produced *Buddenbrooks* (1901) and *The Magic Mountain* (1924). After international acclaim, Mann was awarded the Nobel Prize for Literature in 1929.

The plays of Gerhart Hauptmann, *Before Dawn* (1889) and *The Weavers* (1893), combined naturalism and impressionism. Arno Holz wrote *The Selicke Family* (1892) in collaboration with Johannes Schlaf. The playwright Arthur Schnitzler is known for *Anatol* (1893) and his play about antisemitism, *Professor Bernardi* (1912).

see also...

Naturalism; Realism

Interactive Fiction

While all literature is necessarily interactive, if only because readers respond to texts, interactive fiction is the name given to works in which the author purposefully extends the role of the reader. The writer and reader can explore their relationship if changes are made in the traditional methods of production, design and circulation.

Until recently, interactive texts were constrained because the most efficient method of circulating texts is in print. Challenges to the traditional format of the bound volume include *Hopscotch* (1963) by Julio Cortazar which consisted of 155 unbound chapters for readers to sequence and re-sequence. In 1969, B.S. Johnson's *The Unfortunates* was published in a box as 27 unbound sections. The writer had designated only the first and final segments, the ordering of the rest was left to the reader. *The Dictionary of the Kazars* (1988), by Milorad Pavic, consisted of fictional dictionaries which represented three different cultural traditions.

With the World Wide Web (WWW) on the internet, possibilities for interactivity have multiplied. Authors such as Geoff Ryman (*253,* 1996) have created fictional encyclopedias which can be interrogated like any other database. Some material is now published only electronically. Text-based role-playing games allow users/readers to be involved creatively in the consumption of texts and to influence their development. This is a new form of collaboration, differing from earlier collaborations which usually produced texts created by groups of professional writers.

In some cases, the control of texts has been handed over entirely to readers. Multiple User Dungeons, Object-Oriented (MOO) have allowed the development of virtual writing communities. Experimenting with workshops, collaborations, 'authorless texts', and without editorial control, these websites are based in universities, for example, Nottingham Trent in England and Dallas in the USA.

Irish Revival

Sometimes called the Irish Renaissance, the Irish Revival was an extremely creative period which occurred at the end of the nineteenth century. It grew out of the increasing demand for Irish independence from England and was nationalist in the production of new works and the rediscovery of Gaelic culture. The Gaelic League was founded to promote the language in 1893 and the Irish National Theatre Company was founded in 1899. These key events supported the literary rebirth of Irish writing.

The poet and playwright William Butler Yeats helped to found the theatre with Lady Gregory and Edward Martyn. The first play performed in Dublin was Yeats's *Countess Cathleen* (1892). They later purchased the Abbey Theatre in Dublin where the work of Yeats; John M. Synge (*Playboy of the Western World*, 1907); and Sean O'Casey (*The Shadow of a Gunman*, 1923; *The Juno and the Paycock*, 1924; and *The Plough and the Stars*, 1926), were performed. Other playwrights included Padraic Colum (*The Saxon Shillin'*, 1903) and

Lennox Robinson (*The Lost Leader*, 1918). The plays often starred the brothers William and Frank Fay.

The recreation of Irish myths and legends was important in the literature of this period. Both Yeats (*Collected Poems*, 1950) and Lady Gregory wrote poetry and plays which referred to traditional stories, or took them as starting points for texts which would encourage nationalism. The poems of James Stephens were more realist in style.

The novelist George Moore wrote novels in the styles of naturalism and realism, of which the most famous is *Esther Walters* (1894). The short stories of Liam O'Flaherty, Sean O'Faolain and Frank O'Connor are realist tales which describe the lives of ordinary people in Ireland, their suffering and their lack of opportunity.

These writers had only limited influence on the work of their contemporaries, James Joyce and Samuel Beckett but, in the next generation, Brendan Behan (*The Quare Fellow*, 1959), followed the tradition.

Jazz Age

The social revolution which occurred in the USA immediately following the First World War and the cultural changes which resulted have caused the period to be known as the Jazz Age or the Roaring Twenties. A generation of young men had fought in Europe and had returned home with new ideas, an understanding of the brevity of life and an unwillingness to return quietly to their former lives.

Writers explored and, in some cases lived, the new philosophy. The USA looked to Europe with its multiculturalism, artistic freedom and history of self-expression and liked what it saw. In the USA, the old culture began to give way to sexual equality and sexual freedom, to pleasure and to living for the moment. The older generation despaired as the young danced to newly popular jazz music, and had fun.

The life and writing of F. Scott Fitzgerald typifies the era. Fitzgerald's short stories and novels, *This Side of Paradise* (1920), *The Great Gatsby* (1925), *Tender is the Night* (1934) and *The Last Tycoon* (1941) are key works. His life was punctuated by episodes of drunkenness, poverty and failure to cope with the physical and financial demands of his lifestyle. Zelda Fitzgerald wrote between the periods of her recurring psychiatric illness.

Dorothy Parker was a drama and literary critic. She chronicled the age in a series of witty and sarcastic books including *Death and Taxes* (1931).

Other writers included journalist and novelist Ring Lardner, who wrote humourously about the period; Gertrude Stein; Alice B. Toklas; and John dos Passos (*USA*, 1938).

James T. Farrell gives a contrasting view. His trilogy based on the character Studs Lonigan (1932–5) describes the life of a poor Irish family. Damon Runyon wrote stories set on New York's Broadway.

see also...

Decadence

Literary Schools and Movements

The distinction between literary movements, schools and groups is one which is hard to draw, and about which there has been little agreement among critics and commentators.

The Oxford English Dictionary suggests that a body of people sharing ideas and working together towards bringing them to fruition can be described as a movement. Inherent in this idea are the assumptions that a set of commonly held beliefs exists, and that some prior agreement has been made about how these may be put into practice. This suggestion of some level of organization, even of membership, in the term, would allow it to be applied to political parties and other organizations. However, the apparent associations which develop among writers as a result of the organic spread of ideas cannot always accurately be described as movements. Some literary 'movements' span not only countries as modernism did, but generations, for example, realism.

Similarly, the use of the word 'school' to describe literary activity would seem to be inappropriate when applied to writers. A school is an institution where formal teaching and learning takes place, yet writers rarely train each other. However, there is a tradition of writers developing skills and building on ideas by studying the published work of others. In this sense, innovative authors or poets can be said to 'school' other writers.

Groups of writers, whether described as schools or movements, have rarely been formally constituted or even physically associated. Some groups have published manifestos, for example, the Dadaists and more recently, the New Puritans. Where the explicit intention is to influence other writers to adopt the same set of beliefs, it could be said that a 'school' had been founded.

On the whole, where writers form groups at all, they tend to do so loosely. It is the literary critics, commentators and academics who spot and describe trends and developments and place writers and texts within them.

Lyric

yric was the name given by the ancient Greeks to the verses and poems written to be sung, often by a chorus, to the accompaniment of the lyre. This was an instrument with up to 15 strings, which were plucked. Lyrics were usually short, simple expressions of a poet's feelings and were often based on myths. Early lyric writers were Pindar and Sappho, whose poems concerned her life on the island of Lesbos with a group of young women.

The Romans also used this form. Catullus revived Greek forms in his poems and odes and influenced later poets, including Horace. Horace's book *Ars Poetica,* or *The Art of Poetry,* was rediscovered in Europe during the Renaissance and led to another revival of the lyric form.

There was a simultaneous development of popular song, alongside the lyric. Songs covered topics not included in the more formal lyric. The Roman Empire brought both the lyric form and popular song to Europe. Popular song survived through the Dark and Middle Ages. The European Renaissance revived the ancient forms, and verses written for music were increasingly seen as separate from written or spoken poems. In England, the greatest age of the lyric was the sixteenth century, and examples can be seen in the songs included in the plays of William Shakespeare.

In the nineteenth century, the work of the Romantic poets was based on the classical lyric. The Romantics modernized the content by emphasizing the poet's difficulty in finding a way to express thought and feelings, rather than the simplicity of the process. The *Lyrical Ballads* (1798) of William Wordsworth and Samuel Taylor Coleridge were the first of the longer modern lyric poems. This development can also be seen in the work of Charles Baudelaire (*Les Fleurs Du Mal,* 1867).

Today, the words of songs are still called lyrics and any poetry with a musical quality is described as lyrical.

see also...

Romanticism

Magical Realism

The term magical realism was coined in Germany by Franz Roh in 1925 to describe a movement towards new objectivity in German literature.

The style was later adopted by mainly Latin American Hispanic writers and includes novels by many prominent writers, including Nobel Prize winners. The Argentinian Jorge Luis Borges wrote *A Universal History of Infamy* (1935) and *Labyrinths* (1962). In Columbia, Gabriel Garcia Marquez published *One Hundred Years of Solitude* (1967), the story of one Columbian family which is an allegorical history of Columbia. The Cuban Alejo Carpentier, spent many years in Europe and draws on European as well as South American literary traditions. He wrote *The Lost Steps* (1953) and *Reasons of State* (1974). More recently, Isabel Allende has written *The House of the Spirits* (1982) and *The Enduring Spirit* (1998).

The style has also become popular in Europe. Jose Saramago, the Portuguese Nobel Prize winner in 1988, published *The Year of the*

Death of Ricardo Reis (1984). Some critics have discovered elements of magical realism in the works of the German writer Gunter Grass and the Italian novelist Italo Calvino.

In Britain during the 1970's and 1980's, three writers were particularly noted for their magical realism style: Emma Tennant, Angela Carter and Salman Rushdie. In *Midnight's Children* (1981), Rushdie tells the story of modern India from the perspective of a child born on the stroke of independence.

The characteristic which unites these novels is a blending of the realistic with the fantastic. Elements of the improbable are treated rationally, in the same way as the more ordinary aspects of the narrative, as they are in fairy tales. The result is a complex mingling of the actual and the imaginary, of the explicable and inexplicable, and of myth, dream and legend.

see also...

Fantasy Fiction

Melodrama

Melodrama – in France melodrame – was a term originally used by Jean Jacques Rousseau to describe his play *Pygmalion* (1776), which used music as a background for the dialogue. This differed from opera, where the words are joined to or set to the music. The word melodrama derives from the Greek word *melos*, meaning song, so melodrama was literally a play with songs and music.

Most new melodramas involved conflict between innocence and experience or good and evil, often personified by a helpless young girl and a moustached villain. The heroine was rescued eventually by a fearless hero who usually had a comic friend. After a series of elaborately staged adventures, the duo defeated the villain and the hero married the girl. The genre differs from tragedy because the victims in melodrama are not even partly responsible for their own problems or downfall, but are truly the victims of external forces.

The first melodrama performed in England was *A Tale of Mystery* (1802) by Thomas Holcroft and was a translation of a French play in which two lovers are separated by a villain. The new cities formed during the Industrial Revolution had large populations in search of entertainment. This new form of popular culture met the need with romantic, sensational, emotionally engaging and exciting stories. The genre rapidly became successful throughout Europe, as it was lively, entertaining and accessible to mostly illiterate audiences.

During the nineteenth century August von Kotzebue wrote and produced melodramas in Berlin, and Dionysius Boucicault produced melodramas in London and America, notably *The Colleen Bawn* (1860). Aspects of the genre were incorporated into other literary forms. There are passages of pure melodrama in the novels of Charles Dickens, for example, the death of Little Nell in *The Old Curiosity Shop* (1841).

see also...

Victorian Literature

Metaphysical

Samuel Johnson first used the term 'metaphysical poets' long after the poets he described as such had died. Their contemporaries knew the style as 'strong lined'. During the sixteenth century, poetry was expected to contain difficult ideas expressed concisely. The reader is held to a line of argument by a closely woven text. The use of ellipsis, staccato rhythms, abrupt openings and allusions make the poetry demanding for readers. Consequently, poetry was beyond the reach of most people and was rarely published, but read aloud at gatherings or privately circulated in manuscript form.

Metaphysical poetry was concerned with developing extraordinary perspectives on ordinary events, for example, falling in love or prayer. Poets considered the relationship between the spirit and the senses and expressed this in concrete rather than abstract terms. Allegory was popular, as was the 'conceit'. Conceits are ingenious comparisons which stretch metaphor to the limit. Often, comparisons are forced where no logical connection can be made, but the poet's skill leads the reader step by step to accept points of dissimilarity as likenesses and to ignore incongruities. The rationale for using conceits was to persuade the reader to accept the internal or pseudo-logic within the poem until the poet's point has to be conceded by the reader. Despite the complexity of the conceit, the poems were crafted to read as if spontaneously written.

John Donne, George Herbert, Ben Jonson, Richard Crashaw, Henry Vaughan and Andrew Marvell are the major English metaphysical poets. The subjects addressed in the poems are often religious and many deal with crises of faith. Many poems are about the experience and the problems of love. For example, poets may consider relationships where there is a disparity between the ages of the partners, or unrequited love.

see also...

Allegory; Imagery; Symbolism

Modernism

Modernism is a portfolio term used to describe many movements and schools within literature and the arts. These include impressionism, decadence, fauvism, cubism, expressionism, imagism, vorticism, futurism, dadaism, surrealism, aestheticism, and naturalism. The modernist movement originated in Spanish-speaking South America in the late-nineteenth century and is best described as a search for technical excellence, elegance, simplicity and purity of expression. It drew on French Symbolism by incorporating the exotic imagery, musicality, and pessimism of the poetry.

The modernists experimented with new forms. Although the movement later became associated with right- and then left-wing politics, the early modernists did not see themselves as promoting any particular political ideals. The movement spread to Europe and was dominant in literature until the middle of the twentieth century. A unique feature of modernism is that it drew on different influences in every country. This explains the range of movements it influenced.

The Cuban poet Jose Marti (*Ismaelillo*, 1882), the Columbian poet Jose Ascension Silva, the Mexican Najera Gutierrez, and Ruben Dario (*Azul*, 1888) were the poets originally involved in the movement. Modernist poetry is typified by the juxtaposition of images, apparent fragmentation of ideas and repeated allusions to existing works, known as intertextuality. Examples can be found in the work of W.B. Yeats, Ezra Pound and T.S. Eliot.

Novelists experimented with narrative and introduced ellipsis, open endings, enigma, ambiguity, and increasing complexity of plotting and time sequences. Henry James, Joseph Conrad, D.H. Lawrence, Ford Madox Ford and Virginia Woolf all wrote modernist novels.

see also...

Postmodernism

Music

The relationship between different art forms is such that close relationships are often drawn between practitioners. Thus, painters were closely involved with the Bloomsbury Group, German expressionism involved writers, artists and film-makers, and modernism also involved designers and architects. The relationship between music and writing is particularly close. Collaborations between jazz musicians and poets are well documented and are typified by Stan Tracey's suite *Under Milkwood* which was inspired by Dylan Thomas's play (1953).

Writers have produced plays, novels and poems about all kinds of music. Jazz seems to hold a particular fascination for writers, perhaps because of its history, perceived political relationship to mainstream music and its free form. Josef Skvorecky's novel *The Cowards* (1948) is about the fate of jazz musicians in Nazi Germany, and John Clellon Holmes's *The Horn* (1958) is about the musician Charlie Parker. Holmes's experimental style attempted to transfer jazz improvisation styles to the page.

Popular music has often been used as a framework for the discussion of social and cultural change. Both *Absolute Beginners* (1959) by Colin McInnes and *Expresso Bongo* (1961) by Wolf Mankowitz, are about the beginnings of what became youth culture. *Hi Fidelity* (1995) by Nick Hornby considers the impact of popular music on one person's life. *Platinum Logic* (1981) by Tony Parsons, *Espedair Street* (1987) by Iain Banks and *Great Jones Street* (1989) by Don DeLillo are all set in the rock music business. The protagonist in Stella Duffy's detective story, *Beneath the Blonde* (1997), is the lead singer in a band.

Some works take classical music as a focus. These include *Amadeus* (1979) by Peter Shaffer which examines the relationship between Mozart and Salieri and the nature of creativity.

see also...

Lyric; Performance Poetry

Myths, Legends and Fables

Myths are stories with origins rooted in the early quasi-religious beliefs of cultures, and which pre-date the invention of writing. They are passed down as part of the oral tradition of storytelling. Myths usually explain natural events, for example, for the Australian Aboriginal people, the concept 'dreamtime' explains the world before mankind inhabited the earth. Many cultures have such creation myths. Due to the age of these stories and the impossibility of proving that myths are rooted in fact, the word mythological has come to mean imaginary.

Legend has its root in the Latin word *legenda*, meaning things to be read. The term was used after the Romans adopted Christianity and referred to daily monastic readings from the lives of saints and martyrs. Tales were often exciting and bloodthirsty, so the word has come to mean traditional stories with heroic events. There is a sense that the events recounted originally had some basis in fact.

The word fable derives from the Latin *fabula*, meaning a narrative story. The term describes fictional tales, especially those including a moral, or lesson in ethical living. Animals often personify human characteristics, as in the *Fables* by Aesop, (620 BC – 520 BC).

European 'morality plays' of the fifteenth and sixteenth centuries were written as allegories, in which the seven deadly sins and seven virtues demonstrated the battle between good and evil. La Fontaine's *Fables* (1668) drew on the traditions of the Greeks and the morality plays.

During the twentieth century, as colonialism declined, there was an outpouring of ethnic legends and mythologies. Novelists are able to address their own cultural heritage from a non-Christian standpoint, for example, Amy Tan's *The Bonesetter's Daughter* (2001).

see also...

Allegory

Naturalism

Naturalism was a style first seen in France in 1870. It was the synthesis of reactions to new scientific and philosophical theories and the subjectivism of romanticism. Charles Darwin's *The Origin of the Species on the Basis of Natural Selection* (1859), which expounded a mechanism for evolution, and the French philosopher Hippolyte Taine's ideas of social determinism, gave writers a philosophical basis for naturalism.

The belief that the capabilities of human beings are influenced by natural, biological and hereditary factors caused writers to consider the human condition from a scientific basis. Some felt it important to observe and record the activities of the human species in the way that scientists studied and analysed animal behaviour. Just as animals are subject to external factors, for example, food availability, so it was thought that the conditions governing human life could affect the conduct and outcomes of human lives.

Novelists adopted a pseudo-scientific and almost documentary approach to research and writing. They strove to represent life in as accurate, objective and truthful a way as possible. They considered all classes and lifestyles, but the greatest naturalist novels contain such a wealth of detail about the everyday lives of ordinary people that they read almost as social history. From Emile Zola's work *La Fortune des Rougon* (1871), readers became aware of the conditions of the lower classes and the novels are now regarded as both pessimistic and as humanitarian pleas for change. The characters are so constrained by their conditions, that even freewill cannot help them to escape from degradation. It is therefore the responsibility of society to create a set of conditions which will break the vicious circle of deprivation.

Alphonse Daudet, Guy de Maupassant and Joris-Karl Huysmans show the influence of naturalism.

see also...

Realism; Romanticism

Neoclassicism

Neoclassicism is the name given to the fourteenth century revival of ancient Greek and Roman taste and literary styles. The Italian poet Francesco Petrarch believed that great literature could be written only by those who learned to imitate the style and form of the authors of Greek and Roman times. Petrarch revived the epic, eclogue, ode, satire, tragedy, comedy and epigram. Petrarch's *Sonnets to Laura* were published in *The Complete Works* (1544).

During the Renaissance in the sixteenth century, writers felt that a more formal approach to literature was needed. Aristotle's *Poetics* had been newly translated and this was important in the establishing of firm rules for replicating the forms and genres identified by Petrarch. The resulting rules were more strict than those used in classical times and governed form, balance, restraint, reason, clarity and proportion. Works were also required to show unity of design and aim. Drama was governed by the three unities of time, place and action. This meant that plays were to take place in 'real time' and that no action should take place off-stage or merely be reported to characters in the drama. The rules were based on representing what was believed to be natural, which the philosophers of that time regarded as an absolute.

Pierre Corneille's *Le Cid* (1637) was one of the few works to break the rules of unity and caused a controversy. Corneille, Jean Racine and Alexander Pope wrote comedies and heroic tragedies within the rules of the unities. Major English works in the late-seventeenth century include John Dryden's *All For Love* (1677) and in the eighteenth century Joseph Addison's *Cato* (1713).

In 1674, the French critic and poet Pierre Boileau published a translation of an ancient treatise on the sublime. He discovered that the classicists had valued the potential of human ideas and emotions as well as the actuality of human experience. This allowed writers scope to develop all literary forms beyond the rigidity of the Petrarchan conventions.

Neo-realism

Neo-realism was a literary and artistic movement specific to Italy following the Second World War. Italy had been ruled by a fascist government, led by the dictator Benito Mussolini from 1922 until his murder in 1945. Throughout this period, all forms of art were regulated and censored, but after 1945 artistic freedom flourished again. The themes of resistance and regeneration were central to the literary output, as the inhabitants struggled to rebuild, to come to terms with defeat, and to reunite the political factions which had emerged. The post-war Government encouraged political commitment to the rebuilding (impegno) among the population. The neo-realists portrayed post-war Italy in a realistic way, while appealing to the things which Italians held in common, rather than highlighting the fragmentation of the society. The new-realism was partly an attempt to create a new populist national literature, and its practitioners have been criticized for this.

Alberto Moravia had been forced into hiding after the publication of *Time of Indifference* (1929), which criticized fascism. His post-war novels compared the vitality of the post-war Italy with the repression of the earlier period.

Natalia Ginzburg wrote *All Our Yesterdays* (1952), a novel about the resistance, and Beppe Fenoglio wrote short stories based on his experiences as a partisan and a novel, *Perdition* (1954). He later abandoned neo-realism, as did many of his contemporaries. Italo Calvino, who had been a fighter in the resistance movement, documented his experiences in his first novel *The Path to the Nest of Spiders* (1947). Calvino's later works moved towards folk stories, myths and legends.

Neo-realism was an important, if short-lived literary movement. Neo-realist films by Roberto Rosellini, Vittorio de Sica and Luchino Visconti remain popular statements of the aims of neo-realism.

see also...

Gruppe 47; New Wave; Realism

New Puritans

The new puritan manifesto was published in England in 2001, as the introduction to a collection of short stories. A group of 15 prose writers set themselves ten agreed rules which they would adhere to in order to produce truly modern fiction.

New puritan writers are committed to narrative prose as the primary means of expression. Narrative is allowed to develop only with strict temporal linearity, flashbacks and foreshadowing are strictly rejected, and concurrent narratives are also excluded. They see their work as representative of the present and it is realist in intent. Stories are set in the present and any things or persons named within the texts, other than the fictional characters within the narrative, genuinely exist. No products or places are invented, no names of real people changed. This springs from a belief that contemporary literature becomes part of an historical canon, and that it is the duty of the fiction writer to represent the present as realistically as possible. The writers emphasize clarity, purity and textual simplicity. Poetic language and imagery, arcane punctuation and interjections from the author are all avoided in favour of plot development. The morality of the writer is inherent within plot and character, not heard through an additional authorial voice. Writers seemingly reject the literary developments from the end of the twentieth century, especially in genres such as punk and cyberpunk, which seemed to be leading prose writing towards decadence. The new puritans do not write about dysfunction in individuals or society, but about ordinary events and problems which occur in daily life.

Writers include the novelists Geoff Dyer (*Out of Sheer Rage*, 1997), Toby Litt (*Corpsing*, 2000), Ben Richards (*A Sweetheart Deal*, 2000), Scarlett Thomas (*Bright Young Things*, 2000), and Candida Clark (*The Constant Eye*, 2000).

see also...

Realism

New Wave

The term is used to describe a French literary and artistic movement during the 1950's, which influenced the development of novels, drama and film. Alain Robbe-Grillet wrote a treatise, *For a New Novel*, in 1963. He challenged the traditional construction of the novel, saying that conventional narratives create order, which does not exist in real life, and that the dependence on an omnipresent narrator adds to this effect. Narrative and narrator together give events an illusory collective significance, and the work of a novelist is to explore what happens in the space between external reality and what the human mind projects onto reality. Robbe-Grillet argued that novelists should stop ordering and interpreting events for readers and present non-chronological events through the eyes, memory or imagination of the characters themselves. It would thus be possible to evolve an art of appearances, from which social and moral judgements and fixed values would be absent. Robbe-Grillet practised his ideas in several novels. In *Les Gommes* (The Erasers, 1953) the story is told in several versions and in *Le Voyeur* (1955) the story is told from three viewpoints: the narrator, the main character and the reader. He described his book *Last Year at Marienbad* (1961), as a cine-roman and it became a screenplay for Alain Resnais's film of the same name. Robbe-Grillet's *Project for a Revolution in New York* (1970) used scenarios from American B-movies to portray a crime-ridden city. *Les Derniers Jours de Corinthe* (1994) he described as a novelistic memoir.

Nathalie Sarraute's *Tropismes* (1939), was about involuntary movements made by organisms and was written before the new wave. However, Sarraute embraced the new wave in *The Planetarium* (1959). Mauguerite Duras wrote the screenplay for *Hiroshima Mon Amour* (1959). Duras's prose explored simultaneity and interrupted narrative.

see also...
Postmodernism

Nihilism

The word nihilism is derived from the Latin word *nihil*, meaning nothing. Nihilists believed in nothing – they thought that all social structures were constructs founded on lies and that this made all beliefs meaningless. If people were willing to reject all existing institutions, structures and beliefs, they would see the world as it really is. Nihilists' advice to the world was fourfold: (1) reject all ideas of God; (2) annihilate the idea that 'right' can exist; (3) reject all ideas of civilization, property, marriage, morality and justice; and (4) let the pursuit of your own happiness be your only law. Nihilist beliefs were allied to the political philosophy of anarchism, which has a commitment to the overthrow of law and order.

The nihilist movement started in Russia during the late-nineteenth century. The novelist Ivan Turgenev had studied in Europe and witnessed revolutionaries in action. He wrote *Fathers and Sons* (1862), in which the main character, Bazarov, is a nihilist. This novel inspired the anarchist Mikhail Bakhunin to write *The Revolutionary Catechism* (1869), with Sergei Nechayev. The hero has no property, identity or moral attachments and is a terrorist working to revolutionize the world. Bakhunin also wrote many political pamphlets and tracts, claiming that destruction is a creative passion.

In Fyodor Dostoyevsky's novel *The Possessed or The Devils* (1872), he explores political nihilism within a group of revolutionaries whom he caricatures, and the personal spiritual nihilism of the main character, Stavrogin. In *The Brothers Karamazov* (1880), Ivan is a nihilist. Dostoyevsky seeks to reach an understanding of what life is like for those who have lost all faith. Aspects of nihilist philosophy were incorporated into some later schools of philosophical thought and movements, for example, existentialism and Dadaism.

see also...

Dadaism; Existentialism;
Surrealism; Theatre of the Absurd

Novelization

Novelization is the term used to describe a prose work which has been based on a text originally produced in another form. One of the earliest examples of this is *Tales From Shakespeare* (1807) by Charles and Mary Lamb. In this collection, the plays of William Shakespeare were retold as children's stories, partly because it was felt that the plays needed adapting to a simpler form for younger readers, and also to give access to the plays for those who could not attend the theatre.

The modern form of novelization serves a much different purpose, and should really be seen as part of the cinema and television industries. The form has now been subsumed almost wholly into the marketing of films and television programmes and the 'book-of-the-film' as opposed to the 'film-of-the-book', which is simply adaptation, is becoming an increasingly lucrative part of the book market. The concept here is that after a film has been made from an original script or screenplay, a novel is written. The novel follows the action of the film almost exactly and thus novelization is the complete reverse of adapting a book for cinema or television. Novelizations are actually part of the merchandising spin-offs which surround the release of the film or television series which increase the revenue of the film companies.

An example of novelization is the book of the film *A Fistful of Dollars* by Frank Chandler (1972). This book was written some years after the film, which had been made by Sergio Leone in 1964. A more recent example is *The Piano*, published in 1994. Jane Campion first directed the film from her own original idea and screenplay, and then wrote the book, which she based on the action of the film. In the case of *The Piano*, the novelization was actually written by the screenwriter and director of the film. This is not always the case, as can be seen from the graphic novels and books produced following the success of the television series, *The X-Files*.

> ### see also...
> *Adaptations; Graphic Novel*

OuLiPo

This acronym is the abbreviated form of Ouvroir de Litterature Potentielle (Workshop for Potential Literature) founded in France in 1960 by Raymond Queneau. The workshop grew out of the work of Alfred Jarry who wrote the play *Ubu Roi* (1986) and who had developed a style of writing called pataphysics. Pataphysics was defined by its practitioners as the science of imaginary solutions. Solutions were imaginary because the method of working through issues and problems was to apply the logic of the absurd.

The members of OuLiPo were interested in mathematical patterns and rules. They experimented by applying the formal rules of mathematics to writing. Their interest was in what would happen to language and, therefore, to literature if arbitrary constraints were imposed. This challenge to literary conventions led to the invention, or discovery, of new kinds of writing. For example, some pieces were written with words chosen so that the vowels in the whole piece appeared in alphabetical order. Books of scrambled proverbs and palindromes were published. Members of the group felt that they gained freedom by imposing restrictions, and that the resultant texts revealed the surrealism of everyday life.

Raymond Queneau wrote *Exercises in Style* (1947) and *Un Cent Milliard de Poemes* (A Hundred Thousand Poems) (1961). Georges Perec wrote *La Disposition* (1969), using a device called the lipogram. In this novel every letter 'e' was excluded. The book, translated by Gilbert Adair, was published in English in 1994 as *A Void*. In 1972, Perec wrote *Les Revenentes* (The Return of the 'e') in which the only vowel used is 'e'. Perec also wrote *La Vie: Mode d'emploi* (Life: A User's Guide, 1978). Harry Mathews was the only American member of the group. His work was based on mathematical patterns. These include *Cigarettes* (1987) and *The Journalist* (1994).

see also...

Concrete Poetry; Theatre of the Absurd

Parody

A parody is a piece which is written in imitation of either an existing text or the style of another writer, or both. The intention of the parodist is to amuse the reader by exaggerating the style and the perceived weaknesses of the original writer or specific piece targeted. The first parodies were created in ancient Greece, with the intention of changing or perverting the meanings of the original pieces. An early example of parody is *Frogs* by Aristophanes, which parodies the styles and political beliefs of two other play-wrights, Aeschylus and Euripides.

Famous parodies in English literature include Henry Fielding's *Shamela* (1741), which parodies the best-selling *Pamela* (1740–1) by Samuel Richardson. *Tristram Shandy* (1759–67) by Laurence Sterne is a parody of what was at the time an emerging form, the novel. Sterne's work is a comment on the development of the prose narrative of other writers, and he deliberately makes use of interruption of both time and narrative to humorous effect.

The tradition of parody can be traced through all forms of literature to the present day. Lewis Carroll's poem *Father William,* parodies a poem of the same name by the Poet Laureate of England, Robert Southey. Sir Max Beerbohm wrote *A Christmas Garland* (1912), which parodies the styles of Henry James and Rudyard Kipling. In 1930, Stella Gibbons's *Cold Comfort Farm* imitated the styles of Mary Webb and D. H. Lawrence and their morbid stories set in rural England. The playwright Tom Stoppard wrote *The Real Inspector Hound* in 1968, which parodies the detective story or thriller style of plays of the 1940s.

Examples of parody can still be found in the work of the English poet Martin Newell. Modern parodic pieces are now more likely to be short journalistic or novelty pieces, and of a less enduring quality than those listed above.

> ### see also...
> Comedy and Tragicomedy; Satire

Performance Poetry

Performance poetry is written specifically for performance before a live audience. The American Kenneth Roxroth is credited with introducing modern performance poetry during the 1950s. His intention was to create conditions in which a broader audience could experience poetry. His solution was to take poetry out of the libraries and bookshops and to lift it off the page by performing it. Roxroth achieved success and inspired new poets. The challenge to the usually academic, sometimes dull, image of poetry made performance poetry an accessible form of expression and links were formed with underground poetry.

Although performance poetry is published, the publication and design are of less importance than the performance. A variety of venues are used, including comedy clubs and music venues. The performances are different in style and content from the poetry readings favoured by conventional poets. Poems are recited from memory and the emphasis is on the audience's experience. Performance skills are central to the event and sometimes poetry is accompanied by music.

In the USA, there were close links with Jazz poetry and the beat movement. This can be seen in the work of James Langston Hughes, Kenneth Patchen, Amiri Bakara and Gill Scott Heron. In Britain, Pete Brown and Spike Hawkins worked within this tradition.

In the 1960s, Adrian Mitchell and Michael Horovitz promoted performance poetry in Britain. During the 1980s there was a new wave of performance poets. Some came from a musical background, for example, John Cooper Clarke, while others came from the underground movement and minority ethnic groups. These include Linton Kwesi Johnson (*Dread, Beat and Blood*, 1975) and Benjamin Zephaniah (*Propa Propaganda*, 1994).

---

see also...

Beat Generation; Music; Underground Poetry

Post-colonial Literatures

This term is used in Britain to describe writing in English by authors from countries other than Britain and the USA. Post-colonial literature is produced usually by writers from former colonies. The term describes all forms of writing and other cultural production, for example, cinema and television.

The term is used to describe three things: (1) the whole period during a country's history after colonization; (2) the period after independence was regained; or (3) any writing which could be said to be anti-colonial or which is critical of or oppositional to colonialism, whether written during or after colonization.

These uses, while not mutually exclusive, draw attention to the problems of readers' or critics' attempts to categorize writers and writing. For example, while a text may be defined as post-colonial in any of the three senses, texts can also be classified by form (fiction, non-fiction, prose, poetry or play) and also by style or school (for example, symbolist or realist). Empires and colonists impose economic exploitation upon colonies and their peoples. The imposition of the law, religion and language of the conqueror is a by-product of colonization. The resulting impact on the indigenous language and literature of colonized lands is inestimable. Many former colonies have as little written legacy in the languages originally spoken in their countries as the Celts had when the Romans left Britain. As a result, many books are still written in Standard English, though an increasing number of writers now choose to write in non-standard, dialect and Creole English.

The debate about how, or even whether, to define such writing is still open. If the label 'post-colonial' is to be attached to all writing produced in former colonies, or by citizens of or migrants from or to them, then logically it would never be possible to write an Indian or Jamaican novel. Perhaps the key to solving this problem of definition lies within another debate: who has the right to define?

see also...
Ethnic Fiction

Postmodernism

After 1980, the word 'post-modern' was first used to describe literary developments in the aftermath of modernism, that is from the middle of the 1950s onwards. Some critics argue that the concept of postmodern cannot itself exist, as the idea of modernism is firmly placed in a continuing present and that as such modernism constantly updates and replenishes itself.

Writing across all literary forms since the 1950s has shown some patterns and tendencies which have become increasingly dominant in the literary output of western culture. Postmodernist approaches can also be identified in other media forms which depend on narrative, such as television, cinema and advertising. Among these are parody, pastiche, scepticism, irony and fatalism. During the modernist period, writers and artists believed in the power of the arts to improve the human condition. Writers emphasized purpose and depth and, with its seriousness and redemptive qualities, literature was firmly placed within 'high' culture. By comparison, postmodernism can be seen as superficial in content and random in choice of subject. There is often a mixture of references to the features of both 'high' and 'low' culture within a single text.

The influence of the Theatre of Absurd on postmodernist approaches cannot be underestimated. Vladimir Nabokov, Thomas Pynchon and Kurt Vonnegut all write about aspects of the absurd. Jorge Luis Borges employed a device known as metafiction, in which the reader is constantly reminded by the text that it is fiction.

John Fowles, Angela Carter, Julian Barnes and Jeannette Winterson have been described as postmodern writers. The work of some contemporary writers clearly shows links with magical realism. Peter Ackroyd and Salman Rushdie undermine supposed objective knowledge, for example, history, which is a postmodernist approach.

see also...

Magical Realism; Modernism; Theatre of the Absurd

Pre-Raphaelite Brotherhood

The name adopted by a group of revolutionary artists and poets which formed in London in 1848 around the nucleus of William Holman Hunt, John Everett Millais and Dante Gabriel Rossetti. The Brotherhood rejected developments in art and literature since the Renaissance, feeling that art had become artificial and sentimental. They wanted to recapture the simplicity and sincerity of earlier times, that is, before Raphael. They exhibited in London in 1849, and gained the support of John Ruskin. Their work was based on close personal observation of nature, made use of symbolism and often took religious or classical themes as subjects. The group broke up, but after William Morris and Edward Burne-Jones embraced their principles in the late 1850s, there was a short revival. The Pre-Raphaelites attracted criticism and controversy. Charles Dickens called one of Rossetti's paintings 'mean, odious, revolting and repulsive'.

Four issues of a magazine, *The Germ* (1850), were published under the editorship of William Michael Rossetti which stated the aims of the brotherhood as: 'to enforce and encourage an entire adherence to the simplicity of nature'. Influence from the poetry of John Keats and Dante Alighieri caused the Pre-Raphaelites to be regarded as nostalgic and romantic.

One of the best known poets in this group was Christina Rossetti. Her poetry explored melancholy, hopelessness and unrequited love. Her distinctive style of short lines and irregular rhymes can be seen in *Goblin Market and Other Poems* (1862). Dante Gabriel Rossetti's *Poems and Ballads and Sonnets* were published in 1881.

William Morris is best known for his poetry, political writing and textile design. He was a founder member of the Socialist League in 1884 and wrote *A Dream of John Ball* (1888) and *News From Nowhere* (1891).

see also...

Romantic Fiction; Symbolism; Victorian Literature

Proletarian Literature

The forerunners of 1930s proletarian literature were the humanitarian, naturalist and realist writers of the nineteenth century. With the addition of a taste for idealism and rebellion taken from romanticism, proletarian literature reached its pinnacle among American writers in the 1930s. Following the Wall Street Crash in 1929, there was an economic depression. Some writers wanted to create sympathetic portrayals of ordinary working people and the social injustices which they suffered.

This work was within an established tradition. Charles Kingsley (*The Water Babies*, 1863); Harriet Beecher Stowe (*Uncle Tom's Cabin*, 1852); and Emil Zola (*Germinal*, 1885) had all addressed the situation of the poor. Thomas Hood's (*Song of the Shirt*, 1843) and Walt Whitman's (*Leaves of Grass*, 1855) had raised concerns about 'the common man'. Gerhart Hauptman's play *The Weavers* (1892) was about a revolt among workers in Silesia. Hauptman later won the Nobel Prize in 1912. In the early twentieth century, Henry Green (*Living*, 1929); Robert Tressell (*The Ragged Trousered Philanthropists*, 1914); Jack London (*The Iron Heel*, 1908); and Maxim Gorki (*The Mother*, 1906) addressed workers' conditions and the need for reform.

The greatest works from the USA are Upton Sinclair's *The Jungle* (1906); John Steinbeck's *The Grapes of Wrath* (1939) and Clifford Odets's play, *Waiting for Lefty* (1935). Carl Sandberg's poetry is in the tradition of Whitman.

In Europe, writers were more concerned with the rise of Hitler than with the depression, and Ralph Bates's *The Lean Men* (1934) and Ignatio Silone's *Fontamara* (1934) are determinedly anti-fascist. Walter Greenwood's *Love on the Dole* (1933), Storm Jameson's *None Turn Back* (1936), George Orwell's *Coming up for Air* (1939) and *How Green is my Valley* (1940) by Richard Llewellyn were about the British working class.

see also...

Epic Theatre; Naturalism; Realism

Publishing

To publish is literally to make something available to the public. The word is used in relation to newspapers, books, audio tapes, or music. In England it is most often used to describe the circulation of printed material, and a publisher is a person or company whose business is to organize publication.

There are several stages to the publishing process. A writer may produce a piece of work and then seek to publish it, or the work may be commissioned by a publisher. In the case of a commission, the writer usually receives a sum of money before the book is written, called an advance. This is an advance payment of a share of the projected profits which the publisher expects to make on sales. After publication the writer receives a share of the profit for each book sold. This is called a royalty and is paid to the writer as the owner of the copyright on the writing. Copyright laws ensure that the writer holds the sole legal right to reproduce the work and no other person can reproduce the work in any medium without the writer's permission. To do so constitutes a breach of copyright.

After completion, the work is sent to the publisher, where the copy is read and checked for mistakes by an editor. Once copy-edited, the typesetter produces a printed copy as a galley proof which the writer checks. Meanwhile the designer and typesetter produce illustrations and a cover design. The writer receives mock-up pages, page proofs and eventually final proofs of both text and cover. Everything is checked at each stage before the print-run is started. Every book has an international book number (ISBN). The publisher also arranges distribution and publicity.

Most books are published through mainstream publishing houses, though there are many 'little presses' which produce shorter print runs of books targeted at more specific audiences. The process whereby writers pay part or whole of the publication costs is known as 'vanity publishing'.

see also...

Interactive Fiction

Punk and Cyberpunk

The earliest modern recorded uses of the word punk to describe a criminal were in the USA in the 1920s, although earlier meanings had included: worthless, inferior and rotten. The word has since been associated with crime, aggression, violence and nihilism.

During the 1970s, various art forms were described, or described themselves, as 'punk', notably punk rock music. The music of The Clash, Generation X and the Sex Pistols was characterized by a driving, insistent beat, potentially offensive lyrics and the challenging of musical conventions. The fans also called themselves punks and adopted forms of dancing, dress and behaviour which reflected their opposition to mainstream society. *A Clockwork Orange* (1962) by Anthony Burgess and *Do Androids Dream of Electric Sheep?* (1968) by Philip K. Dick. (filmed as *Blade Runner*) portrayed both the philosophy and concerns of the punk generation. Punk literature reflected major interest in music, drug-taking, crime and sex. By the 1980s science fiction was taking account of the new technologies. In William Gibson's novel *Johnny Mnemonic* (1983), an information courier carries data in a micro-chip in his brain. Gibson's book, *Neuromancer* (1984), developed the idea that there is a parallel universe of information to which the new technologies give us access. Gibson portrays this as a threatening, frightening and violent place where the interests of large corporations rule at the expense of the individual. This universe, or cyberspace, takes its name from cybernetics, the science of control systems. Other writers in this genre include Bruce Sterling, Bruce Bethke, and Rudy Rucker.

Cyberpunk developed during the 1980s. The emphasis is on information technology, and the characters show unconventional or nihilistic values. In literary terms it is a fusion of science fiction and crime. Books in this genre are also called technopunk or radical hard science fiction.

see also...

Graphic Novel; Science Fiction

Realism

This movement developed in France during the nineteenth century as a reaction to Romanticism. Realists took their subjects from everyday life and represented them as accurately and objectively as possible, without idealizing or exaggerating situations. Realists often wrote about working class characters and their living conditions and their situations. Detailed descriptions of poverty, hardship and crime were often included. Honore de Balzac and Stendhal were among the first modern novelists to experiment with realism. A manifesto, *Le Realisme* (1857), which explained and justified realism, was published by the novelist Champfleury.

Earlier, writers attempted a more realistic approach to fiction. Daniel Defoe employed aspects of realism in *A Journal of the Plague Year* (1722). Henry Fielding and Tobias Smollett also wrote about the tribulations of ordinary people. By the nineteenth century, most popular novelists were incorporating realism into their work, for example, Charles Dickens, George Eliot, Fyodor Dostoyevsky and Victor Hugo.

Henry James strove to create authentic characters in real situations. Many of his novels deal with the conflict between the older European cultures and the new American culture, symbolized as a conflict between innocence and experience. James is best known for *The Portrait of a Lady* (1881) and *The Wings of the Dove* (1902).

In the twentieth century, readers' expectations for greater realism grew. In some countries this coincided with the extension of free public education. The newly literate did not wish to read books in which their own lives and experiences remained invisible, and authorship became a possibility for more people. The impact of cinema increased demand for realistic representations of society. Realism is now so established that it is difficult to imagine that a manifesto was ever needed.

see also...

Angry Young Men; Feminist Writing; Naturalism

Rites of Passage

Some novels are described as 'rites of passage' works. The description is taken from the practice of marking special events in life with a ceremony or ritual, which symbolically marks the end of one phase and the beginning of the next. For example, babies are welcomed by ceremonies, partnerships are sealed by them, and the dead are remembered and celebrated by them. The concept of 'rites of passage' has traditionally been associated with religious beliefs, and different religions mark major events with ceremonies and rituals according to their beliefs. Increasingly, non-religious and humanist ceremonies are replacing religious ceremonies.

In a rites of passage novel, the main narrative strand is usually concerned with the transformation of one or more of the major characters as they experience events which change the direction of their lives. Such novels often rely on a quest undertaken by the main character. The character's progress towards a goal leads to a moment of clarity. This in itself results in an increased self-knowledge and emotional understanding of themselves and others, thus moving the character into a new phase.

Twentieth-century novels which fall into this category include Joseph Conrad's *Heart of Darkness* (1899) and E.M. Forster's *A Passage to India* (1924). J.D. Salinger's *Catcher in the Rye* (1951) and *To Kill a Mockingbird* (1960) by Harper Lee are examples from America. William Golding's *Lord of the Flies* (1954) and *Rites of Passage* (1980) both present life-changing experiences. *All the Pretty Horses* (1993) by Cormac McCarthy addresses changes in the American west at the beginning of the twentieth century. Graham Swift's *Last Orders* (1996) is about coping with bereavement.

Many late-twentieth century novels by women, members of minority ethnic groups and those writing within post-colonial frameworks have extended the concept of rites of passage beyond the male and colonial experiences. The work of Paula Gunn Allen, Buchi Emecheta and Amy Tan can be read in this context.

Roman-à-clef

This French term can be translated literally as 'a novel with a key'. The stories are often based on, or include, accounts of the lives of real people, sometimes still living. The encoding of such material by using the device of the roman-à-clef allows writers to present the material as fiction, thus avoiding possible prosecution by those to whom reference is made. For the general reader, without the inside knowledge of the writer's life and friends which provides the 'key', these books appear to be ordinary novels.

The earliest example of a roman-à-clef is Madeleine de Scudery's novel, *Ibrahim, ou L'illustre Bassa* (1641), which was ostensibly an historical romance, but the characters were living people. Mrs Delariviere Manley published *The New Atalantis* in 1709. The book included portraits of prominent politicians of the time. Unusually, Mrs Manley published the key to the novel herself.

Benjamin Disraeli was a prolific novelist and was twice Conservative Prime Minister of England. In his novel *Coningsby* (1844), the character of Lord Monmouth is based on the then still living Lord Hertford. The key to the novel was identified and published, but not by Disraeli.

In Aldous Huxley's *Point Counter Point* (1928) two characters are recognizable as satirical portraits of Huxley's friends: the writers D.H. Lawrence, who became Rampion, and John Middleton Murry, who appeared disguised as Burlap.

The Mandarins (1954), a novel by the French feminist Simone de Beauvoir, includes accounts of a long-running argument between the existentialist writers, Jean Paul Sartre and Albert Camus. In real life, the debate about whether the need to act should outweigh the need for individuals to adhere to their philosophical ideals was central to the development of existentialism.

There are few contemporary examples of the roman-à-clef. The style has fallen into disuse as it is not necessary for writers to employ such circumspection.

Romantic Fiction

From Geoffrey Chaucer's *Troilus and Criseyde* (1385), through Jane Austen's novels to Jackie Collins's blockbusters, the themes of romantic fiction have been constant. Novels address our basic need to understand our emotions, particularly love. Writers explore the social conventions of love, and their transgression.

The genre is sometimes described as dealing with the battle of the sexes, and while the novels have traditionally addressed male-female relationships, modern romantic fiction is more complex. As the role of women changes, so do the characters. Goals vary with the historical period of the setting, and with the politics, gender and sexual orientation of the writer.

Early romances addressed women's lack of social power. In Emily Brontë's *Wuthering Heights* (1847), a woman's love is doomed to fail because she is powerless. In Charlotte Brontë's *Jane Eyre* (1847), the heroine overcomes her lack of power and the taming of Mr Rochester restricts his power.

Romance allows women to have adventures, and earlier books offered true escapism. They reflected women's dreams and ambitions rather than real-life possibilities. Characters were often idealized, pushing the boundaries of their allotted social spaces, and reaching their goals. Most often, these goals were work and marriage, with adventures along the way.

Many novels make marriage their happy closure and the most popular from the twentieth century are by Ethel M. Dell, Georgette Heyer and Catherine Cookson. Some romantic novels take the post-marriage reality as their starting point. Most famous of these is Daphne DuMaurier's *Rebecca* (1938), which has Gothic elements. In more modern romances, marriages fail and the woman is set new or different goals. Joanna Trollope's domestic romances reflect this.

see also...

Feminist Writing; Gothic Fiction; Historical Fiction; Romanticism

Romanticism

The Romantic movement was at its height at the end of the eighteenth and beginning of the nineteenth century. During the Enlightenment, writers became observers and reflectors of the world. Writing was formal and convention bound, and writers became craftspeople imposing order on language to create a rational view of the world. The Romantics were concerned about the individual. In the preface to the *Lyrical Ballads* (1798), William Wordsworth and Samuel Taylor Coleridge stated their aims and beliefs. Robert Southey, Wordsworth and Coleridge are sometimes called the 'Lake Poets', as they lived in the Lake District.

Romantics explored the individual's relationship with nature and the world. Heroes were contemplative and either voluntarily isolated or forcibly outcast. Their struggles to reach harmony with nature became the focus of the work. Harmony was often achieved after heroes underwent a symbolic rebirth, reaching understanding by liberating their emotions and feelings, sometimes by sudden trauma. Examples of this can be found in Coleridge's *The Rime of the Ancient Mariner* (1798) and Lord Byron's poems.

Romantic poetry explored relationships with everyday things. The poets found hidden significance in the commonplace and used the imagery and symbolism of nature to express this. The exercise of the imagination was seen as a legitimate way to release creative power. Imagination became a beam of light, revealing insights into the hidden beauty of the world and giving the power to transform it. Percy Bysshe Shelley's work exemplifies this.

Poets revived some forms of medieval literature, especially the ballad, and used ancient myths. John Keats based *Endymion* (1818), on myth. William Blake created a personal mythology, which developed the possibilities of the creative imagination and its potential for prophecy.

see also...
Feminist Writing; Imagery

Satire

The word satire is derived from the Latin word *satira* meaning mixture. The term was applied to poems which mixed description of living people with comment on their actions. The intention was to attack individuals in an amusing way, and often poets used ridicule, sarcasm, mockery or irony to make their point. Satire is thus more of an attitude to be found within the work than a description of either form or content. Satirical works were popular among the ancient Greeks and Romans and have been used as a political weapon for thousands of years. The difference between satire and parody is that satire uses comedy to attack real people, while parody is specifically written to imitate and make fun of literary forms and individual writers.

The public function of satire is to expose folly and cause reform. Satirists address audiences who share the same moral and intellectual beliefs as themselves. From this standpoint of assumed agreement, individuals are targeted and revealed as aberrant and outside the agreed norms of society. The effect on the victims can be devastating.

The greatest satirical poems were written in Europe during the seventeenth and eighteenth centuries. John Dryden satirized English politics in his poem *Absolom and Achitophel* (1682), while in France, the plays of Molière were popular social satires. Alexander Pope satirized aristocratic social conventions in *The Rape of the Lock* (1712). Jonathon Swift's great satire of political systems in *Gulliver's Travels* (1726) the most enduring and popular of these works. Dr Johnson was also an acerbic satirist.

Satire still forms the basis of much comic writing. Some contemporary fantasy and science fiction can be read as satire, although the modern performance style of stand-up comedy is perhaps the closest in spirit to the original writings.

see also...

Comedy and Tragicomedy; Fantasy Fiction; Parody; Science Fiction; Utopias

Science Fiction

Science fiction is based on plausible visions of the future. These can be visions of scientific or technological innovation and advance, of social and political organization, or changes in the natural world. Some writers have used the genre to explore contemporary issues by writing allegorical or satirical stories and novels.

Early science fiction includes Mary Shelley's *Frankenstein* (1818) and *Journey to Centre of the Earth* (1864) by Jules Verne. H.G. Wells invented *The Time Machine* in 1895 and in 1921 the Czech writer Karel Capek invented the humanoid machine, the robot, in *RUR*. By 1932, Aldous Huxley had created *Brave New World*. Olaf Stapledon wrote a series of novels through the 1930s and 1940s, which began with *The First and Last Men* (1930).

During the 1940s and 1950s specialist magazines began publication in Britain and the USA and increased opportunities for short story writers and novelists. Robert Heinlein, A.E. Van Vogt, Arthur C. Clarke, Brian Alldiss, Philip K. Dick and J.G. Ballard were originally published in magazines, and later developed careers as major science fiction novelists.

Since the Second World War, modern writers have increasingly criticized social and political organization. George Orwell's *1984*, published in 1949, can be read as an allegorical critique of Stalinist Russia or as a dystopian vision. The Polish writer Stanislaw Lem wrote *Solaris* (1961) and used science fiction as a disguise for his opposition to the government.

Isaac Asimov wrote over 400 books, the science firmly based in his career as a scientist and mathematician. Doris Lessing writes both political novels and science fiction, as does Ursula le Guin. Both Kurt Vonnegut and Michael Moorcock write science fiction and fantasy, and mainstream novels. Contemporary writers include Octavia E. Butler, Iain M. Banks and Greg Bear.

see also...

Allegory; Fantasy Fiction; Satire; Utopias

83

Short Story

Short story writing is a discrete form of prose writing which requires particular discipline on the part of the writer. The pieces usually have fewer than 10,000 words though most short stories are considerably shorter. A novel normally has at least 100,000 words. Stories are usually published in anthologies, either by one writer or in themed collections featuring many writers. There is also a market for stories in magazines and on the radio. The term was coined by Brander Matthews in 1901.

Short stories are often about one main character with a problem to solve or an achievement to make. The character surmounts a series of obstacles and only after this can resolution be achieved. The character usually undergoes an emotional or spiritual change as part of the process. Given the length limitation of the form, the author must employ great skill in creating a successful short story.

Memorable short stories introduce characters and motivation quickly, with only enough of the character drawn to allow the reader to understand his or her problem and the journey to resolution. Most short stories use only one or two settings. Writers tend to use short and simply phrased sentences to allow readers or listeners to grasp points quickly. Every word must justify its inclusion by propelling the story forward, and writers use sensually and emotionally evocative language. Short stories are written across many genres and subjects and often have a surprise ending or a 'twist in the tail.'

Some of the finest examples of the short story were written in the nineteenth century by Guy de Maupassant (*Ball of Fat*, 1880) and Mark Twain (*Cannibalism in the Cars*, 1906). Classic twentieth-century stories include Damon Runyan's *Guys and Dolls* (1931); F. Scott Fitzgerald's *An Alcoholic Case* (1937); and Ernest Hemingway's *The Short Happy Life of Francis Macomber* (1938). William Burroughs *So Pack Your Ermines* (1960) is an experimental story which illustrates his 'cut-up' method. Modern writers include Joyce Carol Oates and Raymond Carver.

Socialist Realism

Socialist Realism was the official artistic and literary doctrine of the USSR from 1932 onwards. It was adopted by the Central Committee of the Communist Party and imposed upon the Union of Soviet Writers in 1934 at their first congress. The doctrine demanded that writers and artists should depict life in the USSR in a positive light. This would support the struggle for socialism by helping to reform workers' attitudes and educate them about socialism.

Modernist writers such as James Joyce and Franz Kafka were condemned as bourgeois and decadent. Maxim Gorky's novel, *The Mother* (1906), was recommended to writers as a model. Gorky had been exiled before the Bolshevik revolution in 1916, but returned to Russia and ran the Soviet Propaganda Bureau from 1918.

As the country failed to progress economically, the doctrine, which had once insisted on revolutionary realism, was amended to include other demands, including a little less realism. When Josef Stalin thought that writers were falling short of, or dissenting from the doctrine, new guidelines were set. Writers were forced to conform. They created active and healthy heroes with uncompromising revolutionary principles and a tendency towards self-sacrifice.

Sometimes books were amended by the Government to make them acceptable, for example, Mikhail Sholokhov's *Virgin Soil Upturned* (1932). Stalin also used the doctrine to suppress dissident writers, including Boris Pasternak. In 1957 his manuscript for *Dr Zhivago* was smuggled into Italy and published. Pasternak won the Nobel Prize in 1958 and the book was published in Russia in 1988. Osip Mandelstam was exiled after writing a poem which criticized Stalin. Mandelstam's work was published posthumously.

see also...

Banned, Exiled and Imprisoned Writers; Dissidence; Realism

Spies and Secret Agents

In fiction, spies work for foreign countries and secret agents work for the home country. The stories are about threats to national security by whichever foreign power, or political faction within it or connected to it, is portrayed as hostile. Both secret agents and spies are usually seen to operate from patriotism and idealism, though occasionally they operate from self-interest, or because they have been forced to become involved. Double agents operate outside these rules, for they betray their own country by working for both sides. Stories have been set against almost every political backdrop imaginable.

There are few examples of spy novels from the nineteenth century, though James Fenimore Cooper's *The Spy* (1821) tells the story of a double agent. In England, Erskine Childers's *The Riddle of the Sands* (1903), is regarded as the first spy novel. This was followed by a series set in revolutionary France by Baroness Orczy, *The Scarlet Pimpernel* (1905).

By 1909, spy novels were reflecting modern political developments, and national security became an increasingly important issue. William Tufnell le Queux wrote a series of novels which included *Spies of the Kaiser* (1909), and Joseph Conrad's *The Secret Agent* (1907) and John Buchan's *The 39 Steps* (1915), reiterate the threat from abroad. The novels of Sapper feature Bulldog Drummond and his defence of the Empire, in *The Black Gang* (1922).

After the First World War the genre flourished. W. Somerset Maugham (*Ashenden*, 1928); Compton MacKenzie (*Water on the Brain*, 1933); and Eric Ambler's (*The Mask of Dimitrious*, 1939) gave less glamorous accounts of life as a spy. Graham Greene's *Stamboul Train* (1932) and *Ministry of Fear* (1943) are snapshots of espionage and intrigue.

More recently, sales of novels by Frederick Forsyth, Robert Ludlum and Ken Follett show the enduring popularity of the genre.

see also...

Cold War

Stream of Consciousness

Sometimes known as 'interior monologue', stream of consciousness writing allows the reader to follow the thoughts of characters as a story unfolds. The writer attempts to reproduce the free association and randomness of human thought processes, as if inside the mind of the characters. The narrative is a different form from mainstream novels – events may seem to take place simultaneously and apparently random connections are drawn. The texts are often challenging for the reader, who must work hard to establish a clear narrative. More traditional novel forms concentrate on describing the actions and thoughts of characters from an outside perspective.

One of the earliest uses of this technique was by Laurence Sterne who published *Tristram Shandy* between 1759 and 1767. The style was not popular.

When James Joyce wrote *Ulysses* in 1922, he acknowledged the influence of *Les Lauriers Sont Coupees* (1888), by Edouard Dujardin. Joyce took the style to its ultimate, delivering the whole narrative through the eyes of three characters. The action of the novel occurs on one day, and consists entirely of the characters' thoughts as they walk around Dublin. So free is the representation of thought that the final chapter is entirely unpunctuated.

Pilgrimage (1915–38), is a sequence of novels by Dorothy Richardson, where the action takes place in the mind of the heroine. Virginia Woolf developed the style, from including only experimental sections, through to a whole novel, *The Waves* (1931). In the USA, John dos Passos wrote *Manhattan Transfer* (1925), and William Faulkner wrote *The Sound and The Fury* (1929) and *As I Lay Dying* (1930). Both writers used the technique to show the internal conflict of their characters.

see also...

Bloomsbury Group; Modernism; Postmodernism

Structuralism and Post-structuralism

The roots of structuralism lie in France and the work of Ferdinand de Saussure (1857–1913). He adopted a scientific approach to the study of the uses, meanings and structures of language. Saussure identified two elements of language: a structured set of rules (langue) and speech (parole), which results from applying these rules. Saussure said that a sound, which he called a signifier, carries a meaning which communicates the idea of the thing which is spoken of. The thing spoken of is, therefore, signified. Together, signifier and signified, make a sign. Different language groups have reached agreement, or made a set of rules, about which sound signifies which concept, and this varies between languages. Saussure's theories were developed in the 1960s by Roman Jacobson, Claude Levi-Strauss and Louis Althusser.

Roland Barthes studied how language communicates thoughts. He studied how speakers encode information and how listeners decode and understand speech. He called this semiotics, or the science of signs, and suggested that there was an underlying common structure within cultures. Barthes later believed that everything could be decoded and that readers could discover structures and meanings by analysing or 'deconstructing' what they read or saw. He thought that meanings are not fixed, so that the same text can mean different things to different people. Structuralism influenced cultural theorists, who applied its principles to the analysis of literature and moving images.

Jacques Derrida is sometimes called the first post-structuralist. He challenged the use of scientific structures to understand language and emphasized the multiple and changing meanings of signs, to prove that Saussure's 'rules' were often broken. Derrida's beliefs were more libertarian than those of the structuralists. Michel Foucault and Jacques Lacan were also influential.

see also...

New Wave

Surrealism

The surrealist movement was at its height between the First and Second World Wars. The movement was founded in Paris by Andre Breton who published the *Surrealist Manifesto* (1924). Breton had been a Dadaist, but by 1920 had rejected what he saw as the violent tendencies in Dadaism. He produced a second manifesto in 1930 and in 1936 the International Surrealist Exhibition was held in England.

Surrealists attacked rationalism and logic, which they felt had caused the First World War. Influenced by the psychoanalyst Sigmund Freud, Breton wanted to access the human unconscious without using psychiatry. He felt that if both the conscious and the unconscious could be actively used, we could live in a state of 'super-reality' in which poetry was part of life. This would change literature and the arts, philosophy, psychology and politics.

Surrealists sought to release the unconscious and to resolve the separation between dreams, memories and reality. They developed what they called 'automatic processes' of writing and painting, uncontrolled by the conscious mind and intended to release the primitive energy of the brain. The dreamlike quality of the writing and painting was not subject to reason, but to a commitment to record accurately actual thought processes. The resulting work was often seen as bizarre and lacking in artistic and moral constraint.

French surrealist novelists include Andre Breton (*Najda*, 1928), Louis Aragon (*Paris Peasant*, 1926), and Jean Cocteau (*Les Enfants Terribles*, 1930). Poets include Guillame Apollinaire, Paul Eluard and Robert Desnos. The artists Max Ernst, Joan Miro and Salvador Dali were also surrealists. English surrealists included Herbert Read, Roland Penrose, and the filmmaker Humphrey Jennings. Edward Upward's novels featured a surrealist world called Mortmere (*The Railway Accident*, 1969).

see also...

Dadaism; Theatre of the Absurd

Symbolism

The Greek word *symballein* means 'to put together'. Words which put together a sound and an image are symbols. For example, the word 'cross' brings to the mind a symbol of Christianity. On this literal level, a symbol appeals to the intellect only. Poets who became interested in symbolism attempted to create symbols which had additional meanings and which would appeal also to the reader's imagination and feelings. In this way, poets intended to offer a deeper and broader representation of their experiences by using symbolism as a kind of shorthand between their own and readers' minds.

Literary symbolism was intended to suggest to and evoke for the reader a series of implicit meanings and ideas submerged within the language and imagery of the poem. Symbolist poetry appeals to the subconscious mind, not the rational mind, and readers' reactions are therefore subjective. While symbolic meanings cannot be fixed by the poet, as the reader may make associations which were not in the poet's mind, the appropriate choice of language will allow readers to infer meanings and replicate the writer's feelings.

William Shakespeare and the English metaphysical poets, William Blake and William Wordsworth used symbols drawn from nature. The playwright Friedrich von Schiller and Edgar Allen Poe also made extensive use of symbols.

Charles Baudelaire's collection *Les Fleurs du Mal* (1857); Arthur Rimbaud's *Bateau Ivre* (1871); and the works of Paul Verlaine and Stephane Mallarme are the greatest of the French symbolist poems. The dramatist Paul Claudel continued to produce symbolist writing and in the USA, Walt Whitman experimented with the style. In the twentieth century, W.B. Yeats's, T.S. Eliot's, Robert Frost's and Wallace Stevens's symbolic poetry incorporates much private symbolism.

see also...

Imagery; Metaphysical

Theatre of the Absurd

The Theatre of the Absurd developed mainly among European dramatists in the 1950s and 1960s.

In 1942, Albert Camus published a book of essays, entitled *The Myth of Sisyphus*. One essay considered the Greek legend in which Sisyphus was sentenced by the gods to roll a heavy rock to the top of a hill as a punishment. Every time he approached the summit, the weight of the rock would overcome Sisyphus and force him back. The task was impossible to accomplish. Camus took the myth as a symbol of the human condition and his analysis had a great impact on other writers and dramatists.

Playwrights addressed the idea that the world and our lives are fundamentally impossible to understand. Even though we must attempt to impose structure and order on both, this is pointless, for we are always defeated. The absurdists argued that when human beings realize this truth, we suffer from a sense of loss. This makes us bewildered and purposeless. The Theatre of the Absurd was an attempt to show on stage this process of realization and expression of our feelings about it.

The absurdists challenged tradition by using techniques which were new to the legitimate stage. Playwrights used slapstick, acrobatics, mime and other skills which were part of the circus tradition in productions. Plots did not rely on logical narrative development, and were thought by audiences and critics to be meaningless and incomprehensible. An emphasis on repetition and disjointed dialogue portrayed characters' inner struggle to deal with the world and its pointlessness. Nevertheless, we should fight against accepting our situation. Albert Camus, Jean Genet (*The Maids*, 1947), Samuel Beckett (*Waiting for Godot*, 1954) and Eugene Ionescu (*The Chairs*, 1952) are the most well known absurdists. Edward Albee and Harold Pinter also wrote absurdist plays.

see also...
Existentialism; Surrealism

91

Thrillers and Adventures

These are genres of best-selling popular fiction. Modern adventure stories are written in the tradition of G.A. Henty and Rudyard Kipling, who told stirring tales set mostly in the days of the British Empire. In the twentieth century, political maps were redrawn and attitudes changed, but the thrill of adventure still draws readers. Several sub-genres have developed, which include spy and cold war fiction.

Hammond Innes, Alistair Maclean and Neville Shute were all writing adventure stories for adults in the first half of the twentieth century. Wilbur Smith, Gavin Lyall and John Cleary also write within the genre. Terrorism is the subject of an increasing number of novels, for example, Thomas Harris's *Black Sunday* (1975). Leon Uris's *Trinity* (1976) and Tom Clancy's *Clear and Present Danger* (1989) are both set in Northern Ireland. Robert Ludlum and John Grisham write about the tension between the individual and large corporations, often set against a background of corruption. Political thrillers also form a specific sub-genre. *The Manchurian Candidate* (1959) by Richard Condon and Fletcher Kenebel's *Seven Days in May* (1967) are both set in the USA. J.M Coetzee's *Waiting for the Barbarians* (1980) and Gillian Slovo's *The Betrayal* (1992) are set in South Africa during the period of apartheid. The Nigerian writer Ken Saro-Wiwa's novel *The Prisoner of Jebs* (1988) deals with corruption among government officials. Frederick Forsyth's *The Day of the Jackal* (1971) is a thriller about a plot to assassinate the President of France.

In the USA, novels of political intrigue set in and around the White House and American politics are enduringly popular. These include Irwin Shaw's *The Candidate* (1946); Robert Penn Warren's *All The King's Men* (1946); and Joan Didion's *Democracy* (1984). In England, C.P. Snow's *Corridors of Power* (1963) and David Nobbs *House of Cards* (1989) also deal with political administration at the highest level.

see also...

Cold War; Spies and Secret Agents

Tragedy

Originally defined by Aristotle in the fourth century BC in *Poetics*, tragedy describes literary works, especially drama, where events carry characters inexorably towards disaster or death, or both. Aristotle thought that tragedy was the highest form of drama. The classical tradition established a definition of tragedy which assumed shared values and beliefs between writers and audiences. These are necessary to evoke pity, fear and sadness.

By the sixteenth century, a five act structure was standard and the three unities of time, place and action were formally laid down by the Académie Française in the early seventeenth century. Tragic heroes were shown being drawn into events which they failed to survive, partly because of fatal flaws in their own characters.

In England, the sub-genre of revenge tragedy became popular during the reigns of Queen Elizabeth I (1558–1603) and King James I (1603–25). One of the earliest was *The Spanish Tragedy* (1589) by Thomas Kyd. John Webster's plays featured torture, murder and revenge in *The White Devil* (1612) and *The Duchess of Malfi* (1613). Thomas Middleton wrote *Women Beware Women* (1625) and Francis Beaumont collaborated with John Fletcher to write *Philaster* (1609).

Dramatic tragedy was revived in the nineteenth century. Henrik Ibsen wrote realist dramas, often dealing with women in society, for example, *A Doll's House* (1879). August Strindberg's *Miss Julie* (1888) and *The Dance of Death* (1901) dealt with similar issues.

In America, Eugene O'Neill's *The Iceman Cometh* (1946) and Arthur Miller's *Death of a Salesman* (1949) explored the tragedy of the common man. Samuel Beckett addressed the tragedy of the human condition in *Endgame* (1957) and *Happy Days* (1961).

see also...

Comedy and Tragicomedy; Melodrama

Travelling

There is a strong literary tradition of writing novels in which the entire action takes place while the characters are travelling. Some American and European novels evoke a nomadic past which is now lost to most people. Although many of the titles can properly be placed within genres and movements, they are unified by the writers' fascination with journeys. Humankind's economic and social needs, curiosity, wanderlust and desire to develop and use technology are explored in these works. The physical and psychological journeys the characters make is often a symbol of growth.

Early examples include Tobias Smollett's *The Expedition of Humphry Clinker* (1771); Jules Verne's *Around the World in 80 Days* (1873); and *Three Men in a Boat* (1889) by Jerome K. Jerome.

Books set on trains include *Murder on the Orient Express* (1934) by Agatha Christie and *Stamboul Train* (1932) by Graham Greene. Hundreds of poems have been written about railways from Robert Louis Stevenson's *From a Railway Carriage* (1885), to Philip Larkin's *The Whitsun Weddings* (1964). The action of the stage play *Dutchman* (1964) by Amiri Bakara (LeRoi Jones) takes place in a New York subway train.

Herman Melville's *Moby Dick* (1851); Ernest Hemingway's *The Old Man and the Sea* (1952); Thomas Keneally's *Victim of the Aurora* (1977); and Andrea Barratt's *The Voyage of the Narwhal* (1999), all take place on board ship.

In Bertold Brecht's *Mother Courage and her Children* (1939), the family travel around Europe in a cart. Economic migrancy also motivates John Steinbeck's *The Grapes of Wrath* (1939). In *On The Road* (1957) by Jack Kerouac and Louis MacNeice's poem *The Cyclist*, journeys are made for more pleasurable reasons. Carl Shapiro's poem *Auto Wreck* and J.G. Ballard's novel *Crash* (1973), are concerned with the effects of disrupted journeys.

see also...

Rites of Passage

Underground Poetry

Underground poetry is a term used to describe the work of a group of British poets writing between 1950 and 1970. Their work was published from 1959 onwards in the magazine *New Departures*. American avant-garde, underground and beat writers were also first published in England in this magazine. The editors organized live poetry performances and toured shows which included plays, mime, film, jazz, blues, dance and speeches.

'Underground' was outside, beneath and challenging to mainstream culture, politics and society. The movement opposed academia and its values. Poems contained regional and colloquial speech and by 'lifting poetry from the page' and taking performances to clubs, the unemployed and students, underground poets broke conventions. Poets such as Adrian Mitchell, Jeff Nuttall, Tom Pickard, Heathcote Williams and Alexander Trocci who pioneered the idea that a poem is never finished, often changed work during performances. Work was self-published or published by small presses.

The First International Poetry Incarnation, held in London in 1965, was attended by Allen Ginsberg and Lawrence Ferlinghetti. It started a worldwide movement inspired by the oppositional politics of writers, poets and artists.

Some poets followed the American lead of unifying poetry and jazz. Michael Horovitz, Christopher Logue, Spike Hawkins and Pete Brown worked with free-form musicians to produce poems free from literary conventions, matching phrasing to jazz and blues.

Liverpool was central to the development of the movement. The 'Mersey Sound', the Beatles and modern youth culture were rooted in a group of 'public' poets who emerged in 1960. Adrian Henri, Roger McGough and Brian Patten published *The Mersey Sound* (1967) and *The Liverpool Scene* (1967). This group is known as the Liverpool Poets.

see also...

Beat Generation; Performance Poetry

Utopias

Translated literally from the Greek, the word utopia means 'not a place' or 'nowhere'. The imagined nowhere has always been of importance to the human race. The word is usually taken to mean a place which is ideal in the mind of the writer. The opposite, an imaginary place which portrays the writer's personal hell, is called a dystopia. Just as a utopia is an expression of desire, so a dystopia is an expression of fear. Utopias are personal. Many societies have been imagined, and solutions to the problems of the world have been suggested. By implication, present societies would have to be destroyed if new ones were to be created on earth. Some writers have found this too terrible to contemplate, so have set their utopias in an afterlife or on other planets. Utopias are populated by ideal people who have solved the problems of hunger, work, crime, justice, sickness, education, gender roles and the distribution of wealth. It is the author's route to solutions which make utopias compelling.

The earliest utopia is Plato's *The Republic* (360 BC). Later Sir Thomas More created a humanist *Utopia* (1516); Rabelais created an ideal society in *Gargantua and Pantagruel* (1546); and Sir Francis Bacon created *New Atlantis* (1627).

Later novels include Samuel Butler's *Erewhon* (1872); Edward Bellamy's *Looking Backward: 2000–1887* (1888), in which the chief character dreams the future; and William Morris's *News from Nowhere* (1891). Lord Tennyson's poem *The Lotus Eaters* recognizes the drawbacks of utopia. Twentieth century novelists have envisaged the perfect society, including H.G. Wells (*A Modern Utopia*, 1905); James Hilton (*Lost Horizon*, 1933); and Marge Piercy (*Woman on the Edge of Time*, 1979).

Dystopias are portrayed in *We* (1920) by Yevgevny Zamyatin, George Orwell's *1984* (1949) and Aldous Huxley's *Brave New World* (1932).

see also...

Fantasy Fiction; Science Fiction

Victorian Literature

Victoria was Queen of England from 1837 until 1901. Immediate mental images of Victorian times include commercialism and material progress based on developments in science and technology. We also think of authoritarianism in social conventions, industrial relations and religious expression. The rise of the mercantile middle class was achieved by continuing industrial development and the growth of the empire. This maintained economic differences between rich and poor. National identity was symbolized by Britannia, a character of strength, stability and moral and military superiority. The Great Exhibition in 1851 was a manifestation of Victorian self-image and aspirations. Later in the reign, reform, liberalism and humanitarianism became more important. They revealed hypocrisy and greed and threatened social stability.

While writers celebrated the age, most of them did so with some reservation. Charles Dickens, Anthony Trollope, George Gissing and George Meredith had a humanist dimension which was absent from commercialism and imperialism. The situation of women had progressed little, as the works of George Eliot and Charlotte, Emily and Anne Brontë show. Joseph Conrad, George Moore and H.G. Wells lived on in to the twentieth century and adopted more modern styles and ideas.

Poets of the Victorian age include Lord Tennyson, Elizabeth Barrett Browning, Matthew Arnold, Gerard Manley Hopkins and Algernon Charles Swinburne.

Thomas Hardy, and the poets Robert Bridges, A.E. Housman and Rudyard Kipling, spanned the Victorian and modern periods. Their work shows critical support for the achievements and attitudes of the age.

The Irish playwrights George Bernard Shaw and Oscar Wilde gave an opposing view of Victorian society. J.G. Farrells's novel, *The Siege of Krishnapur* (1979), gives an insight into the Victorian mind at the time of the Indian Mutiny.

Vorticism

The Vorticists were a group of European Writers and artists who were linked to the Futurist and imagist movements. Most Vorticist work was produced between 1912 and 1915. Vorticism, like the other movements, was concerned with human energy and the advantages gained from living in an age of mechanization, but it added a dimension which many commentators and critics saw as a celebration of violence. This caused a failure of growth in the movement.

Wyndham Lewis produced and edited a magazine in England from 1914 onwards. In the first edition of *Blast: The Review of the Great English Vortex,* Lewis and the American poet Ezra Pound outlined the aims of the movement. The 'vortex' was a whirlpool of energy, which created ideas and artistic forms, the meanings of which cannot be fixed. Art and literature should be non-representational and abstract. To encourage avant-garde writers to identify as a group, they published lists of writers and artists whom they called the 'blasted' and the 'blessed',

applauding some and condemning others. The vorticists held an exhibition at the Dore Gallery in 1915.

Wyndham Lewis's novels include *The Apes of God* (1930) in which he attacked the Bloomsbury Group, and *The Revenge for Love* (1937). He became associated with the British Fascist Party. Ezra Pound spent his youth in Europe. His early works *Personae* (1909) and *Ripostes* (1912) were in the imagist style. His major cycle of poems, the *Cantos* (1917–70) was influenced by fascism and he was influential on the next generation of poets, including T.S. Eliot.

The sculptor Henri Gaudier-Brzeska made a major contribution to the movement. His history of sculpture praised the energy of primitive art and condemned the formalism and constraint of everything that followed. He was killed in action in 1915.

see also...

Bloomsbury Group; Modernism

War Novels

Writing about the experience of war has dominated modern literature since Stephen Crane's *The Red Badge of Courage* (1895).

Four novels about the First World War are *Three Soldiers* (1921) by John dos Passos; *All Quiet on the Western Front* (1929) by Erich Maria Remarque; Dalton Trumbo's *Johnny Got His Gun* (1939); and *Paths of Glory* (1935) by Humphrey Cobb.

The Spanish Civil War is portrayed in André Malraux's *Days of Hope* (1937); Ernest Hemingway's *For Whom the Bell Tolls* (1941); and Arturo Barea's trilogy *The Forging of a Rebel* (1951).

The Second World War inspired *The Naked and The Dead* (1948) by Norman Mailer and James Jones's *From Here to Eternity* (1951). Different perspectives are offered by Joseph Heller's *Catch 22* (1961) and Kurt Vonnegut's *Slaughterhouse Five* (1969).

British novels about the Second World War include Henry Green's *Caught* (1943); Nicholas Monsarrat's *The Cruel Sea* (1951); and *Bomber* (1970) by Len Deighton. Neville Shute's *A Town like Alice* (1951) is set in Malaya. Patrick Hamilton's *Slaves of Solitude* (1947) is set in London. Modern writing includes *Proud Monster* (1984) by Iain MacMillan; Anne Michaels's *Fugitive Pieces* (1996); and Tobias Woolf's *The Barracks Thief* (1984).

European novels include Simone de Beauvoir's *The Blood of Others* (1948); Heinrich Boll's *The Train was on Time* (1949); Gunter Grass's *The Tin Drum* (1959); and A. Anatoli's *Babi Yar* (1966).

The war in Vietnam inspired Philip Caputo's *In the Forest of the Laughing Elephant* (1991); Boa Ninh's *The Sorrow of War* (1991); and John M. Del Vecchio's, *The 13th Valley* (1983). One novel about the Gulf War is Christopher John Farley's *My Favourite War* (1997).

see also...

Cold War; Spies and Secret Agents; War Poetry

War Poetry

wentieth-century war poetry is within a tradition reaching back to Virgil's *Aeneid*. There are two main strands within the genre, whether the poetry was contemporary or retrospective. The first is celebratory, with glory, heroism and death as the subjects. An example is Alfred, Lord Tennyson's *The Charge of the Light Brigade*. The second strand is less nationalistic, more introverted and considers the effect of war on individuals. Whether the subject is combat, as in Walt Whitman's *Reconciliation*, or waiting as in Thomas Hardy's *A Wife in London* (1899), the recurring theme is personal tragedy.

Twentieth-century wars were better understood by the populations of the combative countries than any earlier wars. They were also the first wars in which the troops were literate. Soldiers became poets and for the first time their work was published before wars ended. First World War poetry typifies this change. In 1914, poets came from the public school educated middle classes, for example, Siegfried Sassoon and

Rupert Brooke. After 1915, poets emerged from other social classes. Wilfred Owen's *Dulce et Decorum Est*, Isaac Rosenberg's *Dead Man's Dump*, and Ivor Gurney's *The Bohemians* reflect the change from enthusiastic support for the war, to protest and finally to sympathy for all involved.

Outstanding soldier poets of the Spanish Civil War include John Cornford (*A Letter From Aragon*); and Miguel Hernandez (*The Wounded Man*).

The Second World War produced many poets, notably Louis Aragon (*The Lilacs and the Roses*); James Applewhite (*News of Pearl Harbour*); and Richard Eberhart (*Fury of Aerial Bombardment*).

Poets of the Vietnam War include Robert Duncan (*Up Rising*); and Denise Levertov (*Overheard in SE Asia*).

see also...

Georgian Poets; Underground Poetry; War Novels

Westerns

he western genre is typically American. It charts the settlement of the continent and changing political attitudes. James Fenimore Cooper's *The Last of the Mohicans* (1826) offers a realistic picture of the frontier. Walter Edmunds's *Drums Along the Mohawk* (1936) is set during the war of independence, with settlers fighting both the native Americans and the English. Countless novels are about the battles to extend the frontier, for example, the stories of Zane Grey, *Riders of the Purple Sage* (1912). The working people of America are portrayed in these novels: soldiers, cowboys, settlers, saloon owners, dancers, law enforcers and outlaws. Some books have the enduring quality of literature while others have been consigned to the bin marked 'pulp fiction'.

Many stories are known to readers from film adaptations. The poet and novelist Frederick Faust wrote under the pseudonym Max Brand. His books still sell, the most famous *Destry Rides Again* (1930), was filmed in 1939. *The Recreation of Brian Kent* (1919) by Harold Bell Wright, was filmed as *Wild Brian Kent* (1936) and later as *The Wild Bunch* (1969). The story follows a group of outlaws in 1914, whose lifestyle has become an anachronism, trying to survive in a world which they no longer understand. *The Tin Star* (1947) by John W Cunningham was filmed as *High Noon*, while Jack Schaefer's *Shane* (1949) and Owen Wister's *The Virginian* (1902) were filmed under their original titles.

Writers have moved with the times and novels are no longer based on the assumption that European settlers had a right to the tribal lands. Louis L'Amour is the author of over 100 novels, the earliest of which were the first to challenge the old view by considering the effects of settlement on Native Americans. E. Annie Proulx's story *Brokeback Mountain* offers a new angle on life on the range, as does Cormac McCarthy's *Border Trilogy* (1992–9).

see also...

Ethnic Fiction; Historical Fiction

Index